William Shakespeare's

Much Ado About Nothing

Text by
Louva Elizabeth Irvine
(M.A., New York Institute of Technology)
Learning-to-Read-Through-the-Arts Instructor
Solomon R. Guggenheim Museum
New York City, New York

Illustrations by
Jerome Press

 Research & Education Association

MAXnotes® for
MUCH ADO ABOUT NOTHING

Printed in the United States of America

Library of Congress Catalog Card Number 96-67409

International Standard Book Number 0-87891-033-6

MAXnotes® is a registered trademark of
Research & Education Association, Piscataway, New Jersey 08854

What **MAXnotes**® *Will Do for You*

This book is intended to help you absorb the essential contents and features of William Shakespeare's *Much Ado About Nothing* and to help you gain a thorough understanding of the work. The book has been designed to do this more quickly and effectively than any other study guide.

For best results, this **MAXnotes** book should be used as a companion to the actual work, not instead of it. The interaction between the two will greatly benefit you.

To help you in your studies, this book presents the most up-to-date interpretations of every section of the actual work, followed by questions and fully explained answers that will enable you to analyze the material critically. The questions also will help you to test your understanding of the work and will prepare you for discussions and exams.

Meaningful illustrations are included to further enhance your understanding and enjoyment of the literary work. The illustrations are designed to place you into the mood and spirit of the work's settings.

The **MAXnotes** also include summaries, character lists, explanations of plot, and section-by-section analyses. A biography of the author and discussion of the work's historical context will help you put this literary piece into the proper perspective of what is taking place.

The use of this study guide will save you the hours of preparation time that would ordinarily be required to arrive at a complete grasp of this work of literature. You will be well prepared for classroom discussions, homework, and exams. The guidelines that are included for writing papers and reports on various topics will prepare you for any added work which may be assigned.

The **MAXnotes** will take your grades "to the max."

Dr. Max Fogiel
Program Director

Contents

> **Each Scene includes List of Characters,
> Summary, Analysis, Study Questions and
> Answers, and Suggested Essay Topics.**

SECTION ONE

Introduction

The Life and Work of William Shakespeare

The details of William Shakespeare's life are sketchy, mostly mere surmise based upon court or other clerical records. His parents, John and Mary (Arden), were married about 1557; she was of the landed gentry, and he was a yeoman—a glover and commodities merchant. By 1568, John had risen through the ranks of town government and held the position of high bailiff, which was a position similar to mayor. William, the eldest son and the third of eight children, was born in 1564, probably on April 23, several days before his baptism on April 26 in Stratford-upon-Avon. Shakespeare is also believed to have died on the same date—April 23—in 1616.

It is believed that William attended the local grammar school in Stratford where his parents lived, and that he studied primarily Latin, rhetoric, logic, and literature. Shakespeare probably left school at age 15, which was the norm, to take a job, especially since this was the period of his father's financial difficulty. At age 18 (1582), William married Anne Hathaway, a local farmer's daughter who was eight years his senior. Their first daughter (Susanna) was born six months later (1583), and twins Judith and Hamnet were born in 1585.

Shakespeare's life can be divided into three periods: the first 20 years in Stratford, which include his schooling, early marriage, and fatherhood; the next 25 years as an actor and playwright in London; and the last five in retirement in Stratford where he enjoyed moderate wealth gained from his theatrical successes. The years linking the first two periods are marked by a lack of information about Shakespeare, and are often referred to as the "dark years."

At some point during the "dark years," Shakespeare began his career with a London theatrical company, perhaps in 1589, for he was already an actor and playwright of some note by 1592. Shakespeare apparently wrote and acted for numerous theatrical companies, including Pembroke's Men, and Strange's Men, which later became the Chamberlain's Men, with whom he remained for the rest of his career.

In 1592, the Plague closed the theaters for about two years, and Shakespeare turned to writing book-length narrative poetry. Most notable were *Venus and Adonis* and *The Rape of Lucrece*, both of which were dedicated to the Earl of Southampton, whom scholars accept as Shakespeare's friend and benefactor despite a lack of documentation. During this same period, Shakespeare was writing his sonnets, which are more likely signs of the time's fashion rather than actual love poems detailing any particular relationship. He returned to playwriting when theaters reopened in 1594, and did not continue to write poetry. His sonnets were published without his consent in 1609, shortly before his retirement.

Amid all of his success, Shakespeare suffered the loss of his only son, Hamnet, who died in 1596 at the age of 11. But Shakespeare's career continued unabated, and in London in 1599, he became one of the partners in the new Globe Theater, which was built by the Chamberlain's Men.

Shakespeare wrote very little after 1612, which was the year he completed *Henry VIII*. It was during a performance of this play in 1613 that the Globe caught fire and burned to the ground. Sometime between 1610 and 1613, Shakespeare returned to Stratford, where he owned a large house and property, to spend his remaining years with his family.

William Shakespeare died on April 23, 1616, and was buried two days later in the chancel of Holy Trinity Church, where he had been baptized exactly 52 years earlier. His literary legacy included 37 plays, 154 sonnets, and five major poems.

Incredibly, most of Shakespeare's plays had never been published in anything except pamphlet form, and were simply extant as acting scripts stored at the Globe. Theater scripts were not regarded as literary works of art, but only the basis for the performance. Plays were simply a popular form of entertainment for all layers of society in Shakespeare's time. Only the efforts of two of Shakespeare's company, John Heminges and Henry Condell, preserved his 36 plays (minus *Pericles,* the thirty-seventh).

Shakespeare's Language

Shakespeare's language can create a strong pang of intimidation, even fear, in a large number of modern-day readers. Fortunately, however, this need not be the case. All that is needed to master the art of reading Shakespeare is to practice the techniques of unraveling uncommonly-structured sentences and to become familiar with the poetic use of uncommon words. We must realize that during the 400-year span between Shakespeare's time and our own, both the way we live and speak has changed. Although most of his vocabulary is in use today, some of it is obsolete, and what may be most confusing is that some of his words are used today, but with slightly different or totally different meanings. On the stage, actors readily dissolve these language stumbling blocks. They study Shakespeare's dialogue and express it dramatically in word and in action so that its meaning is graphically enacted. If the reader studies Shakespeare's lines as an actor does, looking up and reflecting upon the meaning of unfamiliar words until real voice is discovered, he or she will suddenly experience the excitement, the depth, and the sheer poetry of what these characters say.

Shakespeare's Sentences

In English, or any other language, the meaning of a sentence greatly depends upon where each word is placed in that sentence. "The child hurt the mother" and "The mother hurt the child" have opposite meanings, even though the words are the same, simply because the words are arranged differently. Because word position is so integral to English, the reader will find unfamiliar word arrangements confusing, even difficult to understand. Since Shakespeare's plays are poetic dramas, he often shifts from average word arrangements to the strikingly unusual so that the line will conform to the desired poetic rhythm. Often, too, Shakespeare employs unusual word order to afford a character his own specific style of speaking.

Today, English sentence structure follows a sequence of subject first, verb second, and an optional object third. Shakespeare, however, often places the verb before the subject, which reads, "Speaks he" rather than "He speaks." Solanio speaks with this inverted structure in *The Merchant of Venice* stating, "I should be still/ Plucking the grass to know where sits the wind" (Bevington edition, I, i, ll.17-19), while today's standard English word order would have the clause at the end of this line read, "where the wind sits." "Wind" is the subject of this clause, and "sits" is the verb. Bassanio's words in Act Two also exemplify this inversion: "And in such eyes as ours appear not faults" (II, ii, l. 184). In our normal word order, we would say, "Faults do not appear in eyes such as ours," with "faults" as the subject in both Shakespeare's word order and ours.

Inversions like these are not troublesome, but when Shakespeare positions the predicate adjective or the object before the subject and verb, we are sometimes surprised. For example, rather than "I saw him," Shakespeare may use a structure such as "Him I saw." Similarly, "Cold the morning is" would be used for our "The morning is cold." Lady Macbeth demonstrates this inversion as she speaks of her husband: "Glamis thou art, and Cawdor, and shalt be/What thou art promised" (Macbeth, I, v, ll. 14-15). In current English word order, this quote would begin, "Thou art Glamis, and Cawdor."

In addition to inversions, Shakespeare purposefully keeps words apart that we generally keep together. To illustrate, consider Bassanio's humble admission in *The Merchant of Venice*: "I owe you much, and, like a wilful youth,/That which I owe is lost" (I, i, ll. 146-147). The phrase, "like a wilful youth," separates the regular sequence of "I owe you much" and "That which I owe is lost." To understand more clearly this type of passage, the reader could rearrange these word groups into our conventional order: I owe you much and I wasted what you gave me because I was young and impulsive. While these rearranged clauses will sound like normal English and will be simpler to understand, they will no longer have the desired poetic rhythm, and the emphasis will now be on the wrong words.

As we read Shakespeare, we will find words that are separated by long, interruptive statements. Often subjects are separated from verbs, and verbs are separated from objects. These long interruptions can be used to give a character dimension or to add an element of suspense. For example, in *Romeo and Juliet* Benvolio describes both Romeo's moodiness and his own sensitive and thoughtful nature:

> I, measuring his affections by my own,
> Which then most sought, where most might not be found,
> Being one too many by my weary self,
> Pursu'd my humour, not pursuing his,
> And gladly shunn'd who gladly fled from me.
> (I i,ll 126-130)

In this passage, the subject "I" is distanced from its verb "Pursu'd." The long interruption serves to provide information which is integral to the plot. Another example, taken from *Hamlet*, is the ghost, Hamlet's father, who describes Hamlet's uncle, Claudius, as

> ...that incestuous, that adulterate beast,
> With witchcraft of his wit, with traitorous gifts—
> O wicked wit and gifts, that have the power
> So to seduce—won to his shameful lust
> The will of my most seeming virtuous queen.
> (I,v, ll. 43-47)

From this we learn that Prince Hamlet's mother is the victim of an evil seduction and deception. The delay between the subject, "beast," and the verb, "won," creates a moment of tension filled with the image of a cunning predator waiting for the right moment to spring into attack. This interruptive passage allows the play to unfold crucial information and thus to build the tension necessary to produce a riveting drama.

While at times these long delays are merely for decorative purposes, they are often used to narrate a particular situation or to enhance character development. As *Antony and Cleopatra* opens, an interruptive passage occurs in the first few lines. Although the delay is not lengthy, Philo's words vividly portray Antony's military prowess while they also reveal the immediate concern of the drama. Antony is distracted from his career and is now focused on Cleopatra:

> ...those goodly eyes,
> That o'er the files and musters of the war
> Have glow'd like plated Mars, now bend, now turn
> The office and devotion of their view
> Upon a tawny front.... (I, i, ll. 2-6)

Whereas Shakespeare sometimes heaps detail upon detail, his sentences are often elliptical, that is, they omit words we expect in written English sentences. In fact, we often do this in our spoken conversations. For instance, we say, "You see that?" when we really mean, "Did you see that?" Reading poetry or listening to lyrics in music conditions us to supply the omitted words, and it makes us more comfortable reading this type of dialogue. Consider one passage in *The Merchant of Venice* where Antonio's friends ask him why he seems so sad and Solanio tells Antonio, "Why, then you are in love" (I, i, l. 46). When Antonio denies this, Solanio responds, "Not in love neither?" (I, i, l. 47). The word "you" is omitted but understood despite the confusing double negative.

In addition to leaving out words, Shakespeare often uses intentionally vague language, a strategy which taxes the reader's attentiveness. In *Antony and Cleopatra*, Cleopatra, upset that Antony is leaving for Rome after learning that his wife died in battle, convinces him to stay in Egypt:

> Sir, you and I must part, but that's not it:
> Sir you and I have lov'd, but there's not it;
> That you know well, something it is I would—
> O, my oblivion is a very Antony,
> And I am all forgotten. (I, iii, ll. 87-91, emphasis added)

In line 89, "...something it is I would" suggests that there is something that she would want to say, do, or have done. The intentional vagueness leaves us, and certainly Antony, to wonder.

Though this sort of writing may appear lackadaisical for all that it leaves out, here the vagueness functions to portray Cleopatra as rhetorically sophisticated. Similarly, when asked what thing a crocodile is (meaning Antony himself who is being compared to a crocodile), Antony slyly evades the question by giving a vague reply:

> It is shap'd, sir, like itself, and it is as broad as it hath breadth. It is just so high as it is, and moves with it own organs. It lives by that which nourisheth it, and, the elements onc out of it, it transmigrates.
> (II, vii, ll. 43-46)

This kind of evasiveness, or double-talk, occurs often in Shakespeare's writing and requires extra patience on the part of the reader.

Shakespeare's Words

As we read Shakespeare's plays, we will encounter uncommon words. Many of these words are not in use today. As *Romeo and Juliet* opens, we notice words like "shrift" (confession) and "holidame" (a holy relic). Words like these should be explained in notes to the text. Shakespeare also employs words which we still use, though with different meaning. For example, in *The Merchant of Venice* "caskets" refer to small, decorative chests for holding jewels. However, modern readers may think of a large cask instead of the smaller, diminutive casket.

Another trouble modern readers will have with Shakespeare's English is with words that are still in use today, but which mean something different in Elizabethan use. In *The Merchant of Venice*, Shakespeare uses the word "straight" (as in "straight away") where we would say "immediately." Here, the modern reader is unlikely to carry away the wrong message, however, since the modern meaning will simply make no sense. In this case, textual notes will clarify a phrase's meaning. To cite another example, in *Romeo and Juliet*, after Mercutio dies, Romeo states that the "black fate on moe days doth depend" (emphasis added). In this case, "depend" really means "impend."

Shakespeare's Wordplay

All of Shakespeare's works exhibit his mastery of playing with language and with such variety that many people have authored entire books on this subject alone. Shakespeare's most frequently used types of wordplay are common: metaphors, similes, synecdoche and metonymy, personification, allusion, and puns. It is when Shakespeare violates the normal use of these devices, or rhetorical figures, that the language becomes confusing.

A metaphor is a comparison in which an object or idea is replaced by another object or idea with common attributes. For example, in *Macbeth* a murderer tells Macbeth that Banquo has been murdered, as directed, but that his son, Fleance, escaped, having witnessed his father's murder. Fleance, now a threat to Macbeth, is described as a serpent:

> There the grown serpent lies, the worm that's fled
> Hath nature that in time will venom breed,
> No teeth for the present. (III, iv, ll. 29-31, emphasis added)

Similes, on the other hand, compare objects or ideas while using the words "like" or "as." In *Romeo and Juliet*, Romeo tells Juliet that "Love goes toward love as schoolboys from their books" (II, ii, l. 156). Such similes often give way to more involved comparisons, "extended similes." For example, Juliet tells Romeo:

> 'Tis almost morning, I would have thee gone
> That lets it hop a little from his hand
> Like a poor prisoner in his twisted gyves,
> And with silken thread plucks it back again,
> So loving-jealous of his liberty.
> (II, ii, ll. 176-181, emphasis added)

An epic simile, a device borrowed from heroic poetry, is an extended simile that builds into an even more elaborate comparison. In *Macbeth*, Macbeth describes King Duncan's virtues with an angelic, celestial simile and then drives immediately into another simile that redirects us into a vision of warfare and destruction:

> ...Besides this Duncan
> Hath borne his faculties so meek, hath been
> So clear in his great office, that his virtues
> Will plead like angels, trumpet-tongued, against
> The deep damnation of his taking-off;
> And pity, like a naked new-born babe,
> Striding the blast, or heaven's cherubim, horsed
> Upon the sightless couriers of the air,
> Shall blow the horrid deed in every eye,
> That tears shall drown the wind....
> (I, vii, ll. 16-25, emphasis added)

Shakespeare's employs other devices, like synecdoche and metonymy, to achieve "verbal economy," or using one or two words to express more than one thought. Synecdoche is a figure of speech using a part for the whole. An example of synecdoche is using the word boards to imply a stage. Boards are only a small part of the materials that make up a stage, however, the term boards has become a colloquial synonym for stage. Metonymy is a figure of speech using the name of one thing for that of another which it is associated. An example of metonymy is using crown to mean the king (as used in the sentence "These lands belong to the crown"). Since a crown is associated with or an attribute of the king, the word crown has become a metonymy for the king. It is important to understand that every metonymy is a synecdoche, but not every synecdoche is a metonymy. This rule is true because a metonymy must not only be a part of the root word, making a synecdoche, but also be a unique attribute of or associated with the root word.

Synecdoche and metonymy in Shakespeare's works is often very confusing to a new student because he creates uses for words that they usually do not perform. This technique is often complicated and yet very subtle, which makes it difficult for a new student to dissect and understand. An example of these devices in one of Shakespeare's plays can be found in *The Merchant of Venice*. In warning his daughter, Jessica, to ignore the Christian revelries in the streets below, Shylock says:

> Lock up my doors; and when you hear the drum
> And the vile squealing of the wry-necked fife,
> Clamber not you up to the casements then. . ."
> (I, v, ll. 30-32)

The phrase of importance in this quote is "the wry-necked fife." When a reader examines this phrase it does not seem to make sense; a fife is a cylinder-shaped instrument, there is no part of it that can be called a neck. The phrase then must be taken to refer to the fife-player, who has to twist his or her neck to play the fife. Fife, therefore, is a synecdoche for fife-player, much as boards is for stage. The trouble with understanding this phrase is that "vile squealing" logically refers to the sound of the fife, not the fife-player, and the reader might be led to take fife as the instrument because of the parallel reference to "drum" in the previous line. The best solution to this quandary is that Shakespeare uses the word fife to refer to both the instrument and the player. Both the player and the instrument are needed to complete the wordplay in this phrase, which, though difficult to understand to new readers, cannot be seen as a flaw since Shakespeare manages to convey two meanings with one word. This remarkable example of synecdoche illuminates Shakespeare's mastery of "verbal economy."

Shakespeare also uses vivid and imagistic wordplay through personification, in which human capacities and behaviors are attributed to inanimate objects. Bassanio, in *The Merchant of Venice*, almost speechless when Portia promises to marry him and share all her worldly wealth, states "my blood speaks to you in my veins..." (III, ii, l. 176). How deeply he must feel since even his blood can speak. Similarly, Portia, learning of the penalty that Antonio must pay for defaulting on his debt, tells Salerio, "There are some shrewd contents in yond same paper/That steals the color from Bassanio's cheek" (III, ii, ll. 243-244).

Another important facet of Shakespeare's rhetorical repertoire is his use of allusion. An allusion is a reference to another author or to an historical figure or event. Very often Shakespeare alludes to the heroes and heroines of Ovid's *Metamorphoses*. For example, in Cymbeline an entire room is decorated with images illustrating the stories from this classical work, and the heroine, Imogen, has been reading from this text. Similarly, in *Titus Andronicus* characters not only read directly from the *Metamorphoses*, but a subplot re-enacts one of the *Metamorphoses's* most famous stories, the rape and mutilation of Philomel.

Another way Shakespeare uses allusion is to drop names of mythological, historical, and literary figures. In *The Taming of the Shrew*, for instance, Petruchio compares Katharina, the woman whom he is courting, to Diana (II, i, l. 55), the virgin goddess, in order to suggest that Katharina is a man-hater. At times, Shakespeare will allude to well-known figures without so much as mentioning their names. In *Twelfth Night*, for example, though the Duke and Valentine are ostensibly interested in Olivia, a rich countess, Shakespeare asks his audience to compare the Duke's emotional turmoil to the plight of Acteon, whom the goddess Diana transforms into a deer to be hunted and killed by Acteon's own dogs:

Duke: That instant was I turn'd into a hart,
           And my desires, like fell and cruel hounds,
           E'er since pursue me.
           [...]
Valentine: But like a cloistress she will veiled walk,
           And water once a day her chamber round....
           (I, i, l. 20 ff.)

Shakespeare's use of puns spotlights his exceptional wit. His comedies in particular are loaded with puns, usually of a sexual nature. Puns work through the ambiguity that results when multiple senses of a word are evoked; homophones often cause this sort of ambiguity. In *Antony and Cleopatra*, Enobarbus believes "there is mettle in death" (I, ii, l. 146), meaning that there is "courage" in death; at the same time, mettle suggests the homophone metal, referring to swords made of metal causing death. In early editions of Shakespeare's work there was no distinction made between the two words. Antony puns on the word "earing," (I, ii, ll. 112-114) meaning both plowing (as in rooting out weeds) and hearing: he angrily sends away a messenger, not wishing to hear the message from his wife, Fulvia: "...O then we bring forth weeds,/

when our quick minds lie still, and our ills told us/Is as our earing."
If ill-natured news is planted in one's "hearing," it will render an
"earing" (harvest) of ill-natured thoughts. A particularly clever pun,
also in A*ntony and Cleopatra,* stands out after Antony's troops have
fought Octavius's men in Egypt: "We have beat him to his camp.
Run one before,/And let the queen know of our gests" (IV, viii, ll. 1-
2). Here "gests" means deeds (in this case, deeds of battle); it is also
a pun on "guests," as though Octavius' slain soldiers were to be
guests when buried in Egypt.

One should note that Elizabethan pronunciation was in
several cases different from our own. Thus, modern readers, especially Americans, will miss out on the many puns based on homophones. The textual notes will point out many of these "lost" puns,
however.

Shakespeare's sexual innuendoes can be either clever or tedious depending upon the speaker and situation. The modern
reader should recall that sexuality in Shakespeare's time was far
more complex than in ours and that characters may refer to such
things as masturbation and homosexual activity. Textual notes in
some editions will point out these puns but rarely explain them.
An example of a sexual pun or innuendo can be found in *The Merchant of Venice* when Portia and Nerissa are discussing Portia's past
suitors using innuendo to tell of their sexual prowess:

> Portia: I pray thee, overname them, and as thou
>   namest them, I will describe them, and
>   according to my description level at my
>   affection.
> Nerissa: First, there is the Neapolitan prince.
> Portia: Ay, that's a colt indeed, for he doth nothing but
>   talk of his horse, and he makes it a great
>   appropriation to his own good parts that he can
>   shoe him himself. I am much afeard my lady his
>   mother played false with the smith.
>   (I, ii, ll. 35-45)

The "Neapolitan prince" is given a grade of an inexperienced
youth when Portia describes him as a "colt." The prince is thought

to be inexperienced because he did nothing but "talk of his horse" (a pun for his penis) and his other great attributes. Portia goes on to say that the prince boasted that he could "shoe him [his horse] himself," a possible pun meaning that the prince was very proud that he could masturbate. Finally, Portia makes an attack upon the prince's mother, saying that "my lady his mother played false with the smith," a pun to say his mother must have committed adultery with a blacksmith to give birth to such a vulgar man having an obsession with "shoeing his horse."

It is worth mentioning that Shakespeare gives the reader hints when his characters might be using puns and innuendoes. In *The Merchant of Venice*, Portia's lines are given in prose when she is joking, or engaged in bawdy conversations. Later on the reader will notice that Portia's lines are rhymed in poetry, such as when she is talking in court or to Bassanio. This is Shakespeare's way of letting the reader know when Portia is jesting and when she is serious.

Shakespeare's Dramatic Verse

Finally, the reader will notice that some lines are actually rhymed verse while others are in verse without rhyme; and much of Shakespeare's drama is in prose. Shakespeare usually has his lovers speak in the language of love poetry which uses rhymed couplets. The archetypal example of this comes, of course, from *Romeo and Juliet*:

> The grey-ey'd morn smiles on the frowning night,
> Check'ring the eastern clouds with streaks of light,
> And fleckled darkness like a drunkard reels
> From forth day's path and Titan's fiery wheels.
> (II, iii, ll. 1-4)

Here it is ironic that Friar Lawrence should speak these lines since he is not the one in love. He, therefore, appears buffoonish and out of touch with reality. Shakespeare often has his characters speak in rhymed verse to let the reader know that the character is acting in jest, and vice-versa.

Perhaps the majority of Shakespeare's lines are in blank verse, a form of poetry which does not use rhyme (hence the name blank) but still employs a rhythm native to the English language, iambic pentameter, where every second syllable in a line of ten syllables receives stress. Consider the following verses from *Hamlet*, and note the accents and the lack of end-rhyme:

> The síngle ánd pecúliar lífe is bóund
> With áll the stréngth and ármor óf the mínd
> (III, iii, ll. 12-13)

The final syllable of these verses receives stress and is said to have a hard, or "strong," ending. A soft ending, also said to be "weak," receives no stress. In *The Tempest*, Shakespeare uses a soft ending to shape a verse that demonstrates through both sound (meter) and sense the capacity of the feminine to propagate:

> and thén I lóv'd thee
> And shów'd thee áll the quálitíes o' th' ísle,
> The frésh spríngs, bríne-pits, bárren pláce and fértile.
> (I, ii, ll. 338-40)

The first and third of these lines here have soft endings.

In general, Shakespeare saves blank verse for his characters of noble birth. Therefore, it is significant when his lofty characters speak in prose. Prose holds a special place in Shakespeare's dialogues; he uses it to represent the speech habits of the common people. Not only do lowly servants and common citizens speak in prose, but important, lower class figures also use this fun, at times ribald variety of speech. Though Shakespeare crafts some very ornate lines in verse, his prose can be equally daunting, for some of his characters may speechify and break into doubletalk in their attempts to show sophistication. A clever instance of this comes when the Third Citizen in *Coriolanus* refers to the people's paradoxical lack of power when they must elect Coriolanus as their new leader once Coriolanus has orated how he has courageously fought for them in battle:

> We have power in ourselves to do it, but it is
> a power that we have no power to do; for if he show us his
> wounds and tell us his deeds, we are to put our tongues into

those wounds and speak for them; so, if he tell us his noble
deeds, we must also tell him our noble acceptance of them.
Ingratitude is monstrous, and for the multitude to be
ingrateful were to make a monster of the multitude, of the
which we, being members, should bring ourselves to be
monstrous members.
(II, ii, ll. 3-13)

Notice that this passage contains as many metaphors, hideous
though they be, as any other passage in Shakespeare's dramatic verse.

When reading Shakespeare, paying attention to characters who
suddenly break into rhymed verse, or who slip into prose after
speaking in blank verse, will heighten your awareness of a
character's mood and personal development. For instance, in
Antony and Cleopatra, the famous military leader Marcus Antony
usually speaks in blank verse, but also speaks in fits of prose (II, iii,
ll. 43-46) once his masculinity and authority have been questioned.
Similarly, in *Timon of Athens*, after the wealthy Lord Timon aban-
dons the city of Athens to live in a cave, he harangues anyone whom
he encounters in prose (IV, iii, l. 331 ff.). In contrast, the reader
should wonder why the bestial Caliban in *The Tempest* speaks in
blank verse rather than in prose.

Implied Stage Action

When we read a Shakespearean play, we are reading a performance text. Actors interact through dialogue, but at the same time
these actors cry, gesticulate, throw tantrums, pick up daggers, and
compulsively wash murderous "blood" from their hands. Some of
the action that takes place on stage is explicitly stated in stage di-
rections. However, some of the stage activity is couched within the
dialogue itself. Attentiveness to these cues is important as one
conceives how to visualize the action. When Iago in *Othello* feigns
concern for Cassio whom he himself has stabbed, he calls to the
surrounding men, "Come, come:/Lend me a light" (V, i, ll. 86-87).
It is almost sure that one of the actors involved will bring him a
torch or lantern. In the same play, Emilia, Desdemona's maidser-
vant, asks if she should fetch her lady's nightgown and Desdemona
replies, "No, unpin me here" (IV, iii, l. 37). In *Macbeth*, after killing

Duncan, Macbeth brings the murder weapon back with him. When he tells his wife that he cannot return to the scene and place the daggers to suggest that the king's guards murdered Duncan, she castigates him: "Infirm of purpose/Give me the daggers. The sleeping and the dead are but as pictures" (II, ii, ll. 50-52). As she exits, it is easy to visualize Lady Macbeth grabbing the daggers from her husband.

For 400 years, readers have found it greatly satisfying to work with all aspects of Shakespeare's language—the implied stage action, word choice, sentence structure, and wordplay—until all aspects come to life. Just as seeing a fine performance of a Shakespearean play is exciting, staging the play in one's own mind's eye, and revisiting lines to enrich the sense of the action, will enhance one's appreciation of Shakespeare's extraordinary literary and dramatic achievements.

Historical Background

The Commedie of much A doo about nothing a booke was entered in the Stationer's Register, the official record book of the London Company of Stationers (booksellers and printers), on August 4, 1600 as a play of *My lord chamberlens men* (Shakespeare's acting company) and stayed (not published) without further permission, to prevent unauthorized publication of this very popular play. This quarto text, generally regarded as having been set from Shakespeare's own manuscript, was the copy used for the First Folio of 1623, which is lightly annotated, with minimal and mostly typographic emendation. Since Will Kempe, the great comic actor who played Dogberry, left the Chamberlain's Men in 1599, it is generally agreed that Shakespeare completed this play no later than 1598–1599. Although scholars have attempted to trace the play's roots to Ariosto's tragedy, *Orlando Furioso*, to Bandello's twenty-second story from the *Novelle*, or to Spenser's poetic work, *The Fairie Queen*, in truth, no play ever existed quite like this one, with its interwoven plots, the wit and verve of Benedick and Beatrice, and the highly inventive comic element of Dogberry and his watch, which gives the Claudio–Hero plot most of its vitality. *Much Ado About Nothing* is a subtler version of *Taming of the Shrew*, transposed from farce to high comedy, and it is the scaffolding upon which *Othello* is built.

Well known and often presented to packed houses before its publication, *Much Ado About Nothing* has not lacked the interest of either producers or reviewers over the last four centuries—it has been popular onstage throughout virtually all of its history. It was performed at court in 1613 for Princess Elizabeth and Frederick, Elector Palantine. David Garrick gave *Much Ado About Nothing* its first performance at Drury Lane on November 14, 1748, playing Benedick brilliantly, and regularly offered it until his farewell performance from the stage in May 9, 1776. Notable presentations in the nineteenth century, when productions tended toward lavish spectacle, include Miss Helen Faucit's personation of Beatrice, noted in the *Manchester Courier* of May 9, 1846 as "a performance of rare beauty" and Henry Irving's "exquisite performance" of Benedick at the Lyceum Theater, noted as having been "given with infinite grace" in the *Saturday Review* of October 21, 1882. Twentieth century renditions have frequently changed the time and locale of the play, with productions as diverse as the American Southwest shoot–em up era, the bicycle–riding Edwardian era and the Teddy Roosevelt era of gramophones and keystone cops. The success of these productions show that the original text is universal enough in appeal and balanced in its composition to withstand these chameleon–like experiments without losing any of its sense.

A. C. Swinburne describes this play as Shakespeare's "most perfect comic masterpiece," and states that "[f]or absolute power of composition, for faultless balance and blameless rectitude of design, there is unquestionably no creation of his hand that will bear comparison with *Much Ado About Nothing*." George Bernard Shaw, on the other hand, while stating that the success of this play "depends on the way it is handled in performance," salutes the Bard as a "great musician" and declares the play "irresistible as poetry" but questions Shakespeare's mastery of "gallant badinage" and dismisses Benedick's wit as "coarse sallies" and Beatrice's wit as "indelicacy," all of which is perhaps more a reflection of the taste of his Victorian time than a true assessment of the play. In the end, the merit of this play rests with its proven ability to continue to touch the hearts and cheer the souls of its audience.

Master List of Characters

Don Pedro—*Prince of Aragon, courtly and conventional. Fearful of his reputation, he is easily duped by his brother's deception. He enjoys matchmaking.*

Leonato—*Governor of Messina and father of Hero, whose conventionality is tested by the depth of his grief.*

Antonio—*Leonato's older brother, who tries to philosophize his brother out of his grief, only to find his own anger stirred.*

Benedick—*Brave, quick-witted and spirited young lord of Padua and a professed misogynist, who will prove his love for Beatrice in a most serious manner.*

Beatrice—*Leonato's niece, whose spirited and merry wit is more than a match for Benedick, and who will, in the end, accept his love and marry him.*

Claudio—*Young lord of Florence, who, easily swayed by outer appearances, revengefully denounces Hero as a wanton on their wedding day.*

Hero—*Leonato's daughter, a chaste and docile maiden, wronged by Don John's slander.*

Margaret and Ursula—*Both gentlewomen attending Hero, Margaret is unwittingly employed in Don John's plot to slander Hero.*

Don John—*Don Pedro's illegitimate brother, an envious and mischief-making malcontent and author of the slander against Hero.*

Borachio and Conrade—*Followers of Don John who assist him in his slander, Borachio is a drunkard.*

Dogberry—*Illiterate master constable, whose love of high-faluting words is only matched by his misuse of them, exposes the slanderous deception, thereby saving Hero.*

Verges—*Headborough, or parish constable, Dogberry's elderly companion.*

Sexton (Francis Seacoal)—*Learned town clerk, recorder of the examination of Conrade and Borachio, who will see past*

Dogberry's bumbling and alert Leonato that his daughter's slanderer has been apprehended.

First Watchman and Second Watchman (George Seacoal)— *Dogberry's assistants, who providentially overhear Borachio describe the details of the deception perpetrated upon Hero.*

Balthasar—*Singer attending Don Pedro, whose out–of–key love song sets the tone of the play.*

Friar Francis—*Priest at the nuptials of Claudio and Hero, who devises a plan to change the hearts of Claudio and Don Pedro and reverse the effects of the slander perpetrated by Don John.*

Messenger to Leonato—*Announcer of the arrival of Don Pedro and his companions.*

Another Messenger—*Calls Leonato to the wedding; alerts Leonato that Don John has been taken.*

Attendants, Musicians, Members of the Watch, Antonio's Son and Other Kinsmen—*Members of the community.*

Summary of the Play

The play is set in and near the house of Leonato, governor of Messina, Sicily. Prince Don Pedro of Aragon with his favorite, Claudio, and Benedick, young cavalier of Padua, as well as Don John, the bastard brother of Don Pedro, come to Leonato's. Claudio instantly falls in love with Hero (her name means chaste), Leonato's only child, whom Don Pedro formally obtains for him. While they wait for the wedding day, they amuse themselves by gulling Benedick and Beatrice (Leonato's niece), verbal adversaries who share a merry wit and a contempt for conventional love, into believing that they are hopelessly in love with each other.

Meanwhile, Don John, an envious and mischief–making malcontent, plots to break the match between Claudio and Hero and employs Conrade and Borachio to assist him. After planting the suspicion in the minds of Claudio and the Prince that Hero is wanton, Don John confirms it by having Borachio talk to Hero's maid, Margaret, at the chamber window at midnight, as if she were Hero. Convinced by this hoax, Claudio and Don Pedro disgrace Hero before the altar at the wedding, rejecting her as unchaste. Shocked by the allegation, which her father readily accepts, Hero swoons away and the priest, who believes in her innocence, intervenes. At his suggestion, she is secretly sent to her uncle's home and publicly reported dead in order to soften the hearts of her accusers as well as lessen the impact of gossip. Leonato is grief–stricken.

Benedick and Beatrice, their sharp wit blunted by the pain of the slander, honestly confess their love for each other before the same altar. Benedick proves his love by challenging his friend, Claudio, to a duel to requite the honor of Beatrice's cousin, Hero. Borachio, overheard by the watch as he boasts of his false meeting with Hero to Conrade, is taken into the custody of Constable Dogberry and clears Hero; but Don John has fled. Her innocence confirmed, her father, satisfied with Claudio's penitent demeanor, directs him to hang verses on her tomb that night and marry his niece, sight unseen, the next morning, which Claudio agrees to do, in a double wedding with Beatrice and Benedict. He joyfully discovers that the masked lady he has promised to marry is Hero. The play ends with an account of Don John being detained by the local authorities.

Estimated Reading Time

Much Ado About Nothing was written to be performed before an audience, without intermission, in less than three hours. Allow your imagination full sway in a straight–through, first reading to grasp the plot and characters. This should take about three hours. To understand the play's nuances, reread it and take note of the usage of each word glossed at the bottom of the text. This should take about one hour per act. Observe how the syntax assigned to each character reveals their pattern of thought. Give yourself enough time to explore the play. While you enjoy the humor, language, and the composition, chuckle along with Shakespeare, at our human vanities,

You can use audiotapes, available at libraries, to follow the text and hear the changing rhythms of verse and prose that this play is famous for. Video taped performances are also available. Study groups may easily read the piece aloud.

Act I

Act I, Scene 1

New Characters:

Leonato: *governor of Messina and father of Hero, a man of manners and hospitality, whose conventionality will be tested by the depth of his grief*

Hero: *Leonato's only child, a docile and conventional young woman, honored for her chastity*

Beatrice: *Leonato's spirited niece, gifted with a brilliant wit and interested in Benedick*

Messenger: *brings news of Prince Don Pedro's victory and approach to Messina*

Don Pedro: *prince of Aragon, who victoriously returns from battle against his illegitimate brother for his throne; Leonato's guest during his stay in Messina and enjoys matchmaking*

Claudio: *young count, Don Pedro's courageous right–hand man, who seeks the hand of Hero; a man who relies on his outer senses, will be duped by Don John into shaming Hero*

Benedick: *quick–witted and spirited young count who, though an avowed misogynist, is attracted to Beatrice*

Balthasar: *musician, an attendant on Don Pedro*

Don John: *Don Pedro's malcontented, illegitimate brother who resents Don Pedro and Claudio and will do anything to cross them*

Summary

The scene takes place before Leonato's house. The messenger informs Leonato that victorious Don Pedro, Prince of Aragon, will arrive shortly with his favorite, Lord Claudio of Florence, who performed courageously in battle. Beatrice asks about Lord Benedick of Padua and learns that he has returned a hero. Don Pedro arrives with his valiant lords, Claudio and Benedick, his attendant, Balthasar, and his bastard brother, Don John. Leonato and Don Pedro exchange niceties and Beatrice outspars Benedick in a spirited word–match during which Benedick calls Beatrice "disdainful" and Beatrice calls Benedick a "pernicious suitor." Leonato invites Don Pedro, Claudio, and Benedick to be his guests during their visit. All exit but Benedick and Claudio.

Claudio confesses his attraction to Hero and his desire to marry her if she be modest. Benedick reveals his attraction to Beatrice, "were she not possessed with a fury," and wonders if there is any man who does not fear his wife will be unfaithful. Don Pedro returns and, hearing of Claudio's love for Hero, attests to her chastity and offers to arrange the marriage, by first wooing Hero (disguised as Claudio), then asking Leonato for her hand. And, Benedick professes both his misogyny and his unwillingness to marry.

Analysis

The exposition advises us that all the players are acquainted. Hero immediately recognizes Beatrice's oblique reference to Benedick as "Signor Mountanto," Leonato refers to the long–standing "merry war betwixt Signor Benedick" and Beatrice, and Claudio confesses his attraction to Hero before leaving for the war. This level of intimacy introduces a mimetic realism, much like that in *Hamlet*—giving credibility to the character's actions and easing their confrontations—that is sustained throughout the play. Approximately 75 percent of the play is written in prose, a style nearer to colloquial speech than verse. Both the prose and the verse sound with the vitality of Shakespeare's musical style.

The mask motif, predominant in this play, is emphasized by Benedick and Beatrice and subtly disguised as clever diatribe in the roles that they assume to hide their obsession with each other.

Fashion imagery, a symbol of appearance versus reality, is introduced as Beatrice states that Benedick "wears his faith but as the fashion of his hat" and Benedick calls "courtesy a turncoat." Their wordspar reveals they are memory–locked, but Shakespeare indicates that their relationship will take a turn for the better by the choice of their names—Benedictus means blessed and Beatrice means blesser.

Beatrice's inquiry about Benedick, though well–seasoned with sarcasm, shows her concern about his welfare as she elicits information about whether he returned safely, if he performed well in battle, and the identity of his present associates. Hero's single line in this scene indicates her modest and retiring nature, builds suspense about her character, and subdues interest in her as emphasis is put on Beatrice, who observes everything around her with a relentlessly playful and unrestrained wit. Benedick momentarily lifts his mask to reveal that his misogyny is assumed as a whetstone for his wit, but closes it quickly.

Claudio suspiciously asks Don Pedro if he praises Hero merely "to fetch [him] in" and Don Pedro protests, both lines serving to initiate a symmetrical pattern which Benedick completes with greater force, stridently using musical imagery in his verbal assaults upon the holy state of marriage, creating an ensemble structure with Claudio and Don Pedro playing his willing straight men.

Since marrying an heiress was a young man's best opportunity, Claudio's first question to Don Pedro is, "Hath Leonato any son, my lord?" Don Pedro's plan, to disguise himself as Claudio in order to win Hero for him at the masked ball, renews the mask motif as a well–intentioned deception. This motif sets the stage for the plot, which turns on a series of misunderstandings and deceptions: a quest for honesty and mutual respect as each character learns to discriminate properly and to estimate everything at its true value. This scene is written in prose up to line 272, then continues in verse.

Study Questions

1. Who was victorious in the battle that preceded the opening of the play?

2. What is the relationship between Don Pedro, Claudio, and Benedick?

3. Why is the speech of Leonato, Don Pedro, and Claudio so rigid? What does their style tell us about their characters?

4. How does Beatrice cover up her concern for Benedick?

5. What simile does Beatrice use to describe Benedick's faith?

6. During their wordspar, what accusations do Benedick and Beatrice hurl on each other?

7. What is the greatest fear of Claudio and Benedick?

8. Have the characters met before?

9. What about Hero is of major concern to Claudio?

10. Which character reveals his misogyny? Is this misogyny real?

Answers

1. Prince Don Pedro of Aragon won the battle.

2. Both Claudio and Benedick fought bravely for the prince.

3. The speech of Leonato, Don Pedro, and Claudio shows their adherence to courtly manners and rituals. Their style betrays an addiction to convention.

4. Beatrice covers her concern for Benedick through her witty downgrading of him.

5. Beatrice states that Benedick wears his faith but as the fashion of his hat.

6. Benedict accuses Beatrice of being disdainful and Beatrice accuses Benedict of being a pernicious lover.

7. Both Claudio and Benedick fear becoming cuckolds.

8. Yes, they have met before.

9. Claudio is concerned about Hero's chastity.

10. Benedick reveals his misogyny. The misogyny is merely a whetstone for his wit.

Suggested Essay Topics

1. Contrast the forms of language used by Leonato, Don Pedro, and Claudio with that of Benedick and Beatrice. Why did

Shakespeare give them differing forms of expression? What do these forms tell you about the nature of the characters and the probable direction the play will take? Who are the least predictable and most predictable characters and why?

2. Shakespeare has introduced the concept of masks, or deception, at the onset of the play. Cite the use of this concept. What information does this give us about the theme of the play?

3. Beatrice masks her concern for Benedick with her wit. What does the dialogue suggest about their prior encounters and future encounters? Use the text to explain.

4. When Claudio asks Benedick about Hero's modesty, Benedick responds by asking whether Claudio wants an honest response or his customary macho response. What does this tell you about Benedick's awareness of his own nature? Using the text, discuss Benedick's answer to Claudio's question.

Act I, Scene 2

New Character:

Antonio: *Leonato's brother*

Summary

In Leonato's house, Antonio advises his brother that his servant overheard the prince, Don Pedro, tell Claudio that he loved Hero and that he would reveal this to her at the dance to be held at Leonato's house that night. And, if she found him suitable, he would request her hand from Leonato. Leonato asks Antonio to convey this information to Hero, so she can also prepare her answer should the report he has just heard be true.

Analysis

Noting which can mean observing, overhearing, and musical notation) is an obvious pun in the title (Elizabethans pronounced

nothing/noting alike) and is central to the major theme of this play: appearance versus reality. This theme is continued by having the conversation between Claudio and Don Pedro overheard by a servant, who repeats it to his master, Antonio, who repeats it to his brother, Leonato, who advises him to repeat it to his daughter, Hero, so she, a commoner, can prepare her response to the prince. This brief scene, written in prose, advises us of the speed with which news travels in Messina and complicates the plot with misinformation based on the servant's partial eavesdropping. Hearsay leads to a number of partings between the characters in this play. The word *ado* in the title may also be a pun on the French word for farewell, *adieu*, so common in usage that we find it in the dialogue of the play. Note that musicians enter to work for Leonato (26).

Study Questions

1. Who overheard the conversation between Claudio and Don Pedro, and where did he hear it?

2. Why does Antonio tell his brother about this conversation?

3. What is the misinformation conveyed in this scene?

4. How quickly does news travel in Messina and in what manner?

5. How did this misinformation probably come about?

6. How is "nothing" used as a pun in the title of this play?

7. Is there any other word used in the title of the play which might also be a pun?

8. What does the action of the scene tell us about hearsay?

9. Leonato prefers to treat the information he received in this scene as a dream. Why?

10. Who will tell Hero the news?

Answers

1. Antonio's servant overheard the information in the orchard.

2. Antonio tells Leonato about this conversation in order to

      prepare him for the situation and give him some time to prepare his answer.

3. The misinformation conveyed in this scene is that the prince is in love with Hero and will ask her hand in marriage for himself.

4. News travels very quickly in Messina and is spread by word-of-mouth.

5. The misinformation of the servant is most likely due to the fact that he heard only part of Don Pedro's and Claudio's conversation.

6. Nothing was pronounced like noting during Elizabethan times.

7. "Ado" may be a pun for *adieu*, the French word for farewell, which characterizes the characters' formal breakups as a result of the misinformation generated in the play.

8. The action of this scene tells us that hearsay is oft repeated.

9. Leonato treats the information he learned in this scene as a dream because it is hard for him to readily accept the reality that the prince is in love with and wants to marry his daughter, a commoner.

10. Leonato directed Antonio, her uncle, to tell Hero of the prince's plans.

Suggested Essay Topics

1. In the text, Leonato refuses Antonio's offer to send for the eavesdropping servant. Why? Does he not wish to enlarge on the report? Does he not wish to seem over–anxious? Does he trust his brother implicitly? Explain.

2. In a town where news travels quickly, who else might the servant tell his report to? Might the town now have two rumored suitors for Hero's hand? What kinds of gossip would this lead to? Compare the way news travels in Messina to the ways in which news travels in your community. Are they similar or different?

Act I, Scene 3

New Characters:

Conrade: *Don John's companion, who assumes the position of advisor*

Borachio: *Don John's companion, recently employed by Leonato, who will play a major role in the slander of Hero*

Summary

We are still at Leonato's house. Conrade greets Don John, only to find him in a foul mood. When he attempts to reason Don John out of his misery, Don John takes a perverse and self-willed stance. Conrade advises Don John that he needs to bide his time, reminding him that he is too recently taken back in Don Pedro's good graces, after having confronted him in battle, before resuming his mischief. Don John insists on following his own course, stating that his plain–dealing villainy is more virtuous than flattery and reveals his bitterness at any expectation of humility on his part. As Conrade suggests that he make use of his discontent, Borachio enters to inform Don John that his brother is being entertained by Leonato and that, while employed at Leonato's, he overheard the prince tell Claudio that he will woo Hero for himself, then give her to him. Envious of Claudio's standing as the prince's right–hand man, Don John engages Conrade and Borachio to help him to destroy the count, and goes to the party.

Analysis

The counterplot to the Hero-Claudio plot is introduced through the mean-spirited character of Don John, illegitimate heir to Prince Don Pedro's throne, revealed with pounding alliterative phrases, "moral medicine" and "mortifying mischief," who, although accepted back into the prince's good graces after challenging his throne, is incapable of any gratitude and marinates in his one–dimensional misery. His hanger-ons, Conrade and Borachio, are willing to assist him in any mischief in order to be in his good graces. Don John's casual use of astrological language in his allusion to Conrade being born under the planet Saturn, a signature of cold ambition and sullenness, indicates its common usage in Shakespeare's time.

We learn that news of the marriage is still being overheard and travelling quickly, and Don John intends to take advantage of it to ruin his adversaries. In contrast to the preceding scenes, the only allusion to music here is Don John's out–of–tune statement that he has decreed "not to sing in my cage." This prose scene shows traces of verse (18–24).

Study Questions

1. How is Don John related to Don Pedro?

2. What is Don John's mood in this scene?

3. Under what planet is Conrade born?

4. What kind of advice does Conrade give Don John?

5. How does Don John respond to Conrade's advice?

6. What information does Borachio bring to Don John?

7. What effect does this information have on Don John?

8. Why are Conrade and Borachio willing to assist Don John?

9. Where does Don John go at the end of the scene?

10. How does Shakespeare use repetition and contrast in this scene?

Answers

1. Don John is Don Pedro's illegitimate brother.

2. Don John's mood is foul, based on his willfulness and impatience.

3. Conrade is born under the planet Saturn.

4. Conrade, hoping to appeal to Don John's ambitions, advises him to stay within the prince's good graces until he is able to devise a solid plan to undo his brother and his court.

5. Don John tells Conrade he has no intention of following anyone's will, even for the sake of flattery, other than his own.

6. Borachio informs Don John that the prince is being entertained at supper at Leonato's, where he will woo Hero for Claudio.

7. Don John, envious of Claudio because he bested him in battle, decides to cross him.

8. Conrade and Borachio agree to help Don John in his deception in order to satisfy their own ambitions, should Don John one day become prince.

9. Don John goes to Leonato's house to join the party given for his brother Don Pedro, and to seek a means of crossing Claudio.

10. In this scene, Shakespeare repeats the motif of noting, or eavesdropping, with Borachio, and contrasts Don John's resentment with Don Pedro's forgiveness. Stylistically, Don John's clipped, obsessive speech is void of any geniality.

Suggested Essay Topics

1. Today, unlike the time about which Shakespeare writes, illegitimacy is accepted. Do you think that Don John has a right to resent the world for being born a bastard? Can you think of any argument that would bring about a change of mind in him? Why do you think Conrade advises him to be patient and to practice flattery?

2. Borachio is revealed as an informer who will aid Don John. What kind of a man do you think he is? Ironically, he accidentally obtained his information while employed as a perfumer at Leonato's house. Why do you suppose this is the method Shakespeare used to convey this information to Don John? How is the word odor used in terms of reputation? Explain.

SECTION THREE

Act II

Act II, Scene 1

New Characters:

Margaret and Ursula: *waiting gentlewomen to Hero*

Summary

While Leonato's household awaits the arrival of the maskers, Beatrice tells us that no man is her match and she advises Hero on how to answer the prince when he seeks her hand. The maskers arrive and we are treated to a variety of deceits as they dance. Don Pedro, pretending to be Claudio, takes Hero aside. Beatrice, pretending that she does not know that she is speaking with Benedick, uses the opportunity to call him a fool. All exit except Don John, Borachio, and Claudio.

Don John and Borachio purposefully mistake Claudio for Benedick and tell him that Don Pedro is in love with Hero and swore he would marry her that night. Claudio, believing their deception, is joined by Benedick who teases him about losing Hero. Claudio leaves and Benedick reflects on his conversation with Beatrice.

Don Pedro, Hero, and Leonato return. Don Pedro assures Benedick that his wooing was on Claudio's behalf. When Claudio and Beatrice return, Benedick exits to avoid Beatrice. Don Pedro announces that he has won Hero for Claudio, and Leonato concurs. When Beatrice leaves, Don Pedro observes that Beatrice would be an excellent wife for Benedick, and enlists Leonato, Claudio, and Hero to aid him in making a match.

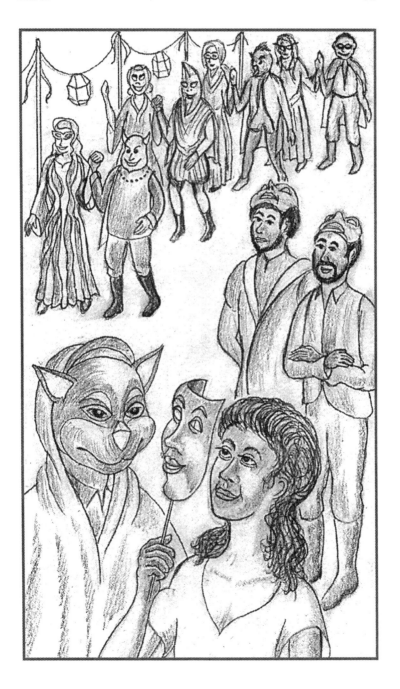

Analysis

The masquerade ball, fashionable in Tudor England, and the guessing game it engenders, emphasizes the problem of knowing/not knowing, which leads to harmony/disharmony. In this scene, Shakespeare offers us both actual music and musical metaphor (Don Pedro teaching birds to sing, i.e., to love).

Claudio's inclination to jealousy and his reliance upon sense information not only leads him to believe Don John's deceit but foreshadows the tragic action he will take at his nuptials. Hero, too proper to do anything but acquiesce in her father's choice, reveals nothing about her feelings for Claudio. Benedick, stung by Beatrice's description of him as little more than a court jester, wonders how she can know him and not know him, ignoring the fact that he said her wit was out of the *Hundred Merry Tales*, a coarse book. The infection of this sting swells toward the end of the scene—when he requests that Don Pedro send him on any absurd mission rather than have three words with Beatrice—and will not be lanced until the end of the act. Beatrice reveals her previous relationship with Benedict when she speaks of his heart (265–68):

> Indeed, my lord, he lent it me awhile; and I gave him
> use for it, a double heart for his single one;
> marry, once before he won it of me with false dice,
> therefore your Grace may well say I have lost it.

Only Don Pedro, dazzled by her lively sallies with him on the topic of marriage, exhibits a flash of intuitive knowledge as he moves past the outer appearance given by Beatrice's mock logic and clever comedy to see her as "an excellent wife for Benedick."

This scene begins and ends with emphasis on Beatrice's unwillingness to consider marriage, which parallels Benedick's diatribe on marriage and sets the tone for the double gulling scenes to come; the counterplot to Beatrice and Benedick's seeming disaffection for each other.

Fashion imagery is continued in this scene. Benedick describes Beatrice as "the infernal Ate" (Greek goddess personifying foolhardy and ruinous impulse) "in good apparel," and Beatrice tells Don Pedro, "[y]our Grace is too costly to wear every day." Note the

appearance of rhymed fourteeners (87–8) and Claudio's speech of 11 lines of end–stopped verse (159–69).

Study Questions

1. To what dances does Beatrice compare wooing, wedding and repenting?

2. Whom does Ursula dance with and how does she recognize him?

3. What statement of Benedick preceded Beatrice's put–down of him during the dance?

4. Whom does Don John purposefully mistake for Benedick?

5. Which characters have soliloquies in this act?

6. Would Benedick marry Beatrice if she were "endowed with all that Adam had left him before he transgressed"?

7. Was Don Pedro able to win Hero for Claudio?

8. When will Claudio and Hero's wedding take place?

9. Whom does Don Pedro think would be an excellent wife for Benedick?

10. Leonato predicts that Benedick and Beatrice, after one week of marriage, will be in what condition?

Answers

1. Beatrice compares wooing to a Scotch jig, wedding to a measure, and repenting to a cinquepace.

2. Ursula is dancing with Antonio, Leonato's brother. She recognizes him by the waggling of his head and the dryness of his hand.

3. Benedick told Beatrice that someone had told him that she was disdainful and had her wit out of the *Hundred Merry Tales.*

4. Don John purposefully mistakes Claudio for Benedick.

5. Claudio and Benedick have soliloquies in this act.

6. No, Benedick would not marry Beatrice, even if she were endowed with all that Adam had left him before he transgressed.

7. Yes, Don Pedro was able to win Hero for Claudio.

8. Claudio and Hero will marry seven days later, on a Monday.

9. Don Pedro thinks that Beatrice would be an excellent wife for Benedick.

10. Leonato predicts that Benedick and Beatrice would, if married but one week, talk themselves mad.

Suggested Essay Topics

1. Why is Claudio so easily deceived by Don John and Borachio? How does he respond to the deception? What does his soliloquy tell you about his character?

2. Using the text, explain what happened off stage during Benedick's dance with Beatrice? How do we know this happened? What effect did this have on Beatrice?

3. What effect did his dance with Beatrice have on Benedick? Does Beatrice know him and not know him? Is there any truth in her statement that he is Don John's court jester? How does he respond to Beatrice afterward? How do you think he'll respond to her in the future? Explain, citing lines from the text.

4. Don Pedro considers Beatrice a good match for Benedick, while Leonato thinks they'll talk themselves to death in a week. Who do you agree with? Why? Use the text to defend your position.

Act II, Scene 2

Summary

Borachio tells Don John that he can cross the marriage of Claudio and Hero. Don John jumps at the opportunity. Borachio lays out his plan to have Margaret, Hero's waiting–gentlewoman, look out her mistress' window the night before the wedding and be mistaken for Hero, while he, Borachio, woos her. He directs Don John to tell Don Pedro that he has dishonored himself by arranging a marriage between Claudio and a common trollop, and then offer him proof of Hero's disloyalty by bringing him to witness the staged deceit. Don John accepts the plan and offers Borachio a fee of a thousand ducats.

Analysis

Borachio, recently employed as a perfumer at Leonato's, is the directive force of this prose scene. Don John, disappointed that his ploy to break the friendship between Don Pedro and Claudio failed, willingly accepts Borachio's plan and direction to destroy the planned marriage of Claudio and Hero, which moves the counter-plot forward and prepares the audience for the crisis to come.

The plan hinges on Don John's ability to persuade Don Pedro that he has dishonored himself, and the coldness of Don John assures us that he will have no second thoughts about implementing this action. His offer of a large fee to Borachio ensures that Borachio will play his part well. Shakespeare emphasizes the sourness of this scene's note by placing it between two musical scenes. At this point the first movement of action, dominated by Don Pedro, in the role of matchmaker, ends and we look forward to seeing the marriage–mockers reformed and the villain defeated.

Study Questions

1. What is the first thing that Borachio tells Don John?

2. Who is the architect of the plan to slander Hero?

3. What does Don John state would be medicinable to him?

4. What did Borachio tell Don John a year ago?

5. What role has been assigned to Don John in this plan?

6. Who will be mistaken for Hero?

7. What role will Borachio play?

8. What effect do the plotters expect to have on the prince, Claudio, Hero, and Leonato?

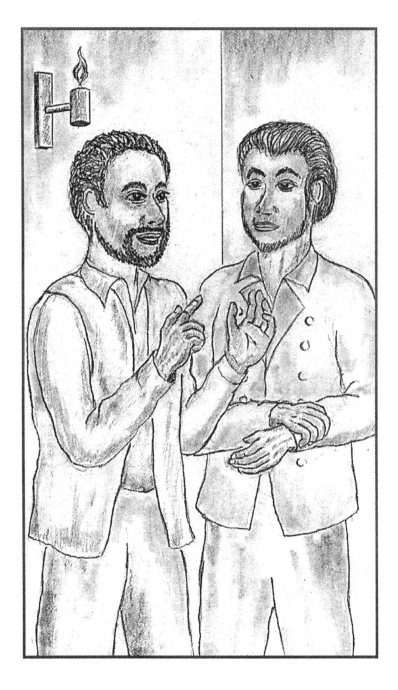

9. How is the only way the plan will succeed?

10. How much will Don John pay Borachio for his deceit?

Answers

1. The first thing Borachio tells Don John is that he can cross the marriage between Claudio and Hero.

2. Borachio is the architect of the plan to slander Hero.

3. Don John states that any cross, any impediment to the marriage of Claudio would be medicinable to him.

4. Borachio told Don John that he is in the favor of Margaret, Hero's waiting-gentlewoman.

5. Don John's role is to first plant the slander in Don Pedro's mind and then to offer him proof.

6. Margaret will be mistaken for Hero.

7. Borachio will play the role of Hero's lover.

8. The plotters intend to misuse the prince, to vex Claudio, to undo Hero, and to kill Leonato.

9. The plan will only succeed if Don John can first convince Don Pedro that his honor has been sullied by arranging the alliance between Claudio and Hero.

10. Don John will pay Borachio a thousand ducats for his deceit.

Suggested Essay Topics

1. Who designed and is directing the slander against Hero? What is the plan? How will it be brought about? What roles have been assigned and to whom? Cite the text to explain.

2. Do you think Borachio's plan will succeed? What do you think the responses of Don Pedro and Claudio are likely to be? Would you fall for such a hoax? Explain.

3. What are the motives of the plotters? Are they the same or different? Can any motive ever justify slander? What values does a slanderer lack? Explain.

Act II, Scene 3

New Character:

Boy: *sent by Benedick to fetch a book*

Summary

The scene takes place in Leonato's garden. Benedick reflects on love and marriage. He hides himself in the arbor when Don Pedro, Leonato, and Claudio enter. Pretending not to note his presence, they listen as Balthasar sings a song about the deceptions of men. Then they speak of Beatrice's love for Benedick, which they claim they learned from Hero. Benedick does not believe it to be a gull because Leonato is involved. They detail the depth of Beatrice's passion and frustration, fearful that she will harm herself because of it, then list her virtues. They agree that Benedick is too scornful to be told of the matter and exit. Reflecting on what he has just heard, Benedict acknowledges to himself his love for Beatrice. Beatrice, sent by Don Pedro to call Benedick to dinner, is perceived by Benedick in a new light as he looks for evidence of her affection for him.

Analysis

The second movement of action, which propels this play into high comedy, begins now and continues through the first scene of Act IV. Highly theatrical, this is Benedick's chief scene in the play, the one his lines have been building toward and the one on which the validity of the rest of his actions depend. The phrasing of the soliloquies, well–written for stage delivery and the actor's memory, require a balanced performance with inventive stage business (player's actions that establish atmosphere, reveal character, or explain a situation) to succeed. The scene takes place in the evening, before supper. It is written in prose except for 21 lines of blank verse spoken by Don Pedro and Claudio (36–56). The new character, the boy, perhaps serves as an image of innocence, or possibly the line was written for the child of one of the company members to play.

Ironically, in Benedick's pre–gulling soliloquy, amply full of his usual self–satisfied, machismo rhetoric, he wonders, for a moment, if he may be so converted as to see with the same eyes of love he has just expressed contempt for. In this moment, Benedick's character initiates a new level of awareness by stepping out from his position as clever onlooker and seeing himself as part of the comedy of human behavior. Although he immediately dismisses the thought, he proceeds to share his ideal woman with us (25–33):

> One woman is fair, yet I am well; another is wise,
> yet I am well; another virtuous, yet I am well; but
> till all graces be in one woman, one woman shall
> not come in my grace. Rich she shall be, that's
> certain; wise or I'll never look on her; mild, or
> come not near me; noble, or not I for an angel; of
> good discourse, an excellent musician and her
> hair shall be of what color it please God.

Shakespeare references and thereby emphasizes the title of this play with a musical extension of the pun on "noting" and "nothing" before Balthasar sings a love song, which serves to soften Benedick, although he dismisses Balthasar's singing as a dog's howl. As the gullers proceed to speak of Beatrice's love for him, Benedick's comments about them abate, and he eavesdrops in blank amazement. They cite in her the very virtues he demanded before their arrival. The irony is that Don Pedro, Claudio, and Leonato think they are lying about Beatrice's love for Benedick, when, in fact, they are telling the truth.

In his post–gulling soliloquy, a chastened Benedick steps forward and speaks directly for the first time (217–226):

> This can be no trick. The conference was sadly
> borne. They have the truth of this from Hero. They
> seem to pity the lady. It seems her affections have
> their full bent. Love me? Why, it must be requited.
> I hear how I am censured. They say I will bear
> myself proudly, if I perceive the love come from
> her; they say too that she will rather die than give
> any sign of affection. I did never think to marry. I

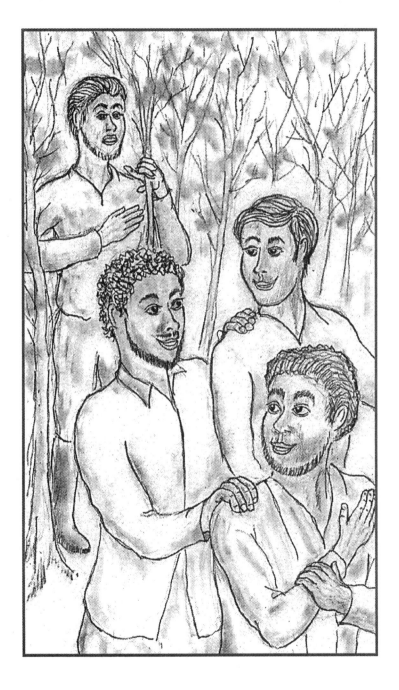

must not seem proud; happy are they that hear
their detractions and can put them to mending.

The passage reveals that Benedick has undergone an attitude adjustment from which he emerges with an expanded conscience, a humbled ego, and an intuitive understanding of his real feelings for Beatrice, then he bursts into his old effusiveness with the declaration that he will love Beatrice "most horribly" and climaxes with the comedic hyperbole, "the world must be peopled." At this point, Shakespeare sends in Beatrice, which heightens the comedic value of the scene as Benedick, a confirmed bachelor turned love fanatic, spies "some marks of love" in her curt speeches. This is a prose scene except for 21 lines of blank verse.

Study Questions

1. What is orthography? Who has turned orthography?

2. What graces does Benedick seek in a woman?

3. To what does Benedick liken Balthasar's singing?

4. When does Shakespeare reference the title of the play?

5. Why does Benedick dismiss the thought that he is being gulled?

6. From whom do the plotters claim to have received their information?

7. Who fears that Beatrice will die and why?

8. How in love with Beatrice does Benedick declare he will be?

9. Did Beatrice call Benedick into dinner on her own initiative?

10. At the end of the scene, what does Benedick spy in Beatrice?

Answers

1. Webster defines orthography as the art of writing words with the proper letters according to standard usage. Claudio has turned orthography.

2. Benedick expects a woman to be rich, wise, virtuous, mild, noble, of good discourse, and an excellent musician.

3. Benedick likens Balthasar's singing to a dog howling.

4. Shakespeare references the title of the play before gulling Benedick.

5. Benedick dismisses the thought that he is being gulled because he does not believe that an elder such as Leonato would be in on such a plot.

6. The plotters claim to have received their information from Hero.

7. Hero fears that Beatrice will die because of her unrequited love for Benedick.

8. Benedick declares that he will be horribly in love with Beatrice.

9. No, she did not. Against her will, Beatrice was sent to call Benedick into dinner.

10. Benedick spies some marks of love in Beatrice at the end of this scene.

Suggested Essay Topics

1. Why do you think Shakespeare chooses the moment of Benedick's gulling to remind us of the title of the play? Why does he use flattery to ensnare Benedick? Is Benedick actually misled by the gull or does the gull offer him the opportunity to own a part of himself he had denied? Explain.

2. Compare Benedick's two soliloquies. Do they reveal a change in consciousness? Describe the change in consciousness, citing the text.

3. How are Benedick's speeches, before and after the gulling, handled stylistically? Do they have theatrical value? Explain, citing specific passages from the play. How do you imagine an actor would play this role? Describe specific stage business the actor would employ.

Act III

Act III, Scene 1

Summary

The scene takes place in the garden. Hero sets the trap for Beatrice by sending Margaret to tell Beatrice that she is the subject of Hero and Ursula's gossip. Beatrice appears instantly and follows them, hidden among the honeysuckle, to eavesdrop. Hero and Ursula speak of Benedick's unrequited love for Beatrice and Beatrice's disdainful scorn for Benedick. They speak of Benedick's virtues and Beatrice's faults, concluding that Beatrice is too self–endeared to be told of the matter. Hero, feigning exasperation, tells Ursula that she will devise some honest slander to poison Benedick's love for Beatrice and thereby save him from wasting away with love. Alone, reflecting on what she has just heard, Beatrice surrenders contempt and maiden pride, determined to accept Benedick's love.

Analysis

A day has passed since the gulling of Benedick. This charming parallel scene is written wholly in verse, most of which is end–stopped, and terminates with a 10-line stanza composed of quatrains and a couplet. We find the usually loquacious Beatrice quietly listening, and you can be sure that any skilled actress will find a variety of attitudes to express in this silence. Surprisingly, quiet and docile Hero mischievously leads the gull. Beatrice's soliloquy shows

her lyric response to their conversation (107–16); it is short and to the point:

> What fire is in mine ears? Can this be true?
> Stand I condemned for pride and scorn so much?
> Contempt, farewell, and maiden pride, adieu!
> No glory lives behind the back of such.
> And Benedick, love on; I will requite thee,
> Taming my wild heart to thy loving hand.
> If thou dost love, my kindness shall incite thee
> To bind our loves up in a holy band;
> For others say thou dost deserve, and I
> Believe it better than reporting.

Through a series of parallels, Shakespeare has brought both Benedick and Beatrice from feigned antipathy to mutual romantic idealism. Beatrice's simple, humble, intuitive acceptance of her faults and her willingness to change foreshadows the intimacy of her next meeting with Benedick.

The scene is short but believable. There is no reason to extend this scene because we know from the first scene of the play that Beatrice's concern for Benedick is real, though guarded due to an earlier perceived rejection by him. Since we've witnessed Benedick's change, we readily accept her change.

Study Questions

1. On whom do Hero and Ursula play the gull?

2. Where is Beatrice during this scene?

3. Who told Hero that Benedick was in love with Beatrice?

4. What character defects does Hero ascribe to Beatrice?

5. How would Beatrice treat a fair–faced man?

6. Why does Hero say it is useless to mention these defects of character to Beatrice?

7. What counsel does Hero intend to give to Benedick?

8. Which scene in the play does this one parallel?

9. How does Cupid kill?

10. Which faults does Beatrice willingly give up in her soliloquy?

Answers

1. Hero and Ursula play the gull on Beatrice.

2. Beatrice is hidden in the honeysuckle arbor.

3. Don Pedro and Claudio told Hero that Benedick was in love with Beatrice.

4. Hero states that Beatrice is disdainful, scornful, and full of intellectual pride.

5. Beatrice would swear that the gentleman be her sister.

6. Hero says that it is useless to mention these defects of character to Beatrice because Beatrice would respond with mockery.

7. Hero intends to counsel Benedick to fight against his passions.

8. This scene parallels the preceding scene, in which Benedick was similarly gulled.

9. Cupid kills some with arrows, some with traps.

10. Beatrice willingly surrenders contempt and maiden pride in her soliloquy.

Suggested Essay Topics

1. Why does Beatrice accept the gull so willingly? Why is she able to surrender her faults so freely? What does this tell you about the true nature of her character? Explain.

2. What does Beatrice mean when she says that "others say thou [Benedick] doest deserve, and I believe it better than reportingly"? What is a better evidence than mere report? Where is it found? Why is this evidence more reliable for Beatrice? Explain.

3. If you were directing this play, how would you manage this scene? What stage business would you give to Beatrice, Hero, and Ursula? What would be the overall tone? Explain fully.

Act III, Scene 2

Summary

It is the night before the wedding. Don Pedro announces he will depart for Aragon right after the nuptials. He refuses Claudio's offer to accompany him. Don Pedro and Claudio observe a change in Benedick, including a shaved face and pristine habits of personal hygiene, and tease him about it. Benedick, unusually sober in demeanor, protests that he has a toothache. He invites Leonato to walk with him in order to enter into a short but private conversation. Don John enters. He tells Don Pedro and Claudio that Hero is disloyal and invites them to go with him to witness her chamber window entered that night at midnight. Claudio vows to shame Hero before the congregation if he witnesses such disloyalty that evening and Don Pedro vows to join him in disgracing Hero.

Analysis

Although this prose scene opens in a relaxed manner, the pacing of the play is speeding up to propel us toward the crisis in Act IV. Claudio's prompt offer to leave with the prince, rather than stay for his honeymoon, indicates that he loves Hero as an image to be possessed rather than as a person to be explored. This does not surprise us since he kept his interest in her on the back burner until the war was over. We see a new and reflective Benedick, unwilling to play court jester and no longer completing Claudio and Don John's lines with witty rejoinders, hidden behind the excuse of a toothache. His memorable line from this scene is "everyone can master a grief but he that has it." Don Pedro and Claudio use clothes imagery to tease clean-shaven, perfumed, and fashionably dressed Benedick, who takes Leonaro offstage for a few short words, presumably about Beatrice, to avoid his friend's jesting. At this point the two harmoniously interwoven major plots begin a polarization, not to be reconciled until the solution, forming a strong dramatic rhythm.

The confusions thrown on the path of the action of the play have prepared us for this moment and the major action of this scene arrives with Don John and unfolds as he puts the scheme to slander Hero into action. Characterized as an observer rather than a participator, he knows exactly how to trap his prey, appealing to Don Pedro's reputation and Claudio's jealousy. He dominates the dialogue, feeding Don Pedro and Claudio their lines, which he completes with deceitful sophistry. The subordinate voice pattern Shakespeare assigned to Don Pedro and Claudio, in which their lines had no meaning unless completed by a third party, now traps them tragically (111–130):

Claudio:	May this be so?
Don Pedro:	I will not think it.
Don John:	If you dare not trust that you see, confess not that you know. If you will follow me, I will show you enough; and when you have seen more and heard more, proceed accordingly.
Claudio:	If I see anything tonight why I should not marry her tomorrow, in the congregation where I should wed, there will I shame her.
Don Pedro:	And, as I wooed for thee to obtain her, I will join with thee to disgrace her.
Don John:	I will disparage her no farther till you are my witnesses. Bear it coldly but till midnight, and let the issue show itself.
Don Pedro:	O day untowardly turned!
Claudio:	O mischief strangely thwarting!
Don John:	O plague right well prevented! So will you say when you have seen the sequel.

Prisoners in Don John's world of sense evidence, they abandon their judgment and adopt his cruel view of the world; Don Pedro and Claudio reflect its emotional scenery as they move into prejudicial and vindictive stances prior to witnessing the evidence. We can easily guess what their response to Don John's hoax will be. The action toward the crisis of the play is now in full spin.

Study Questions

1. When does this scene take place?

2. What is Benedick's observation about grief?

3. Has anyone seen Benedick at the barber's?

4. What does Claudio say about Benedick's jesting spirit?

5. What malady does Benedick claim to have?

6. Who shall be buried with her face upwards?

7. Who invites Leonato to walk aside with him?

8. Why does Don John include Claudio in his conversation?

9. What does Don John tell Don Pedro and Claudio?

10. What invitation does Don John extend to Don Pedro and Claudio?

Answers

1. This scene takes place the night before the wedding.

2. Benedick observes that everyone can master a grief but he that has it.

3. No. But the barber's man has been seen with Benedick.

4. Claudio says that Benedick's jesting spirit is now crept into a lute string and now governed by stops.

5. Benedick claims to suffer from a toothache.

6. Beatrice will be buried with her face upwards.

7. Benedick invites Leonato to walk aside with him.

8. Don John includes Claudio in his conversation because the matter he speaks of concerns him.

9. Don John tells Don Pedro and Claudio that Hero is disloyal.

10. Don John invites Don Pedro and Claudio to witness Hero's disloyalty with their own eyes and ears.

Suggested Essay Topics

1. What does the change in Benedick's dialogue and demeanor tell us about Benedick? Why will he no longer play the fool? What few words does he wish to have with Leonato? What

does this indicate about the stance his character will take in the future?

2.   Why was Don John so easily able to plant suspicion about the chastity of Hero in the minds of Don Pedro and Claudio? What does this tell us about their characters? What do you imagine will be their reaction when they see the staged deceit? Describe the probable scene.

3.   Stylistically, what syntactic pattern does Shakespeare use to trap Don Pedro and Claudio in Don John's deceit? What does this pattern tell you about the character's thinking habits? Why was it effective? Explain.

Act III, Scene 3

New Characters:

Dogberry: *illiterate master constable, whose love of high–faluting words is only matched by his misuse of them, he exposes the slanderous deception, thereby saving Hero*

Verges: *headborough, or parish constable, Dogberry's elderly companion*

First Watchman and Second Watchman (George Seacoal): *Dogberry's assistants, who providentially overhear Borachio describe the details of the deception perpetrated upon Hero*

Summary

The scene takes place at night, on the street, to the side of the door of Leonato's house. Master Constable Dogberry, bearing a lantern, and his elder compartner, Verges, arrive with the watch. Dogberry gives them their charge, specifically instructing them to watch about Leonato's door because of the preparations for the marriage. Borachio staggers forth from Leonato's, followed by Conrade, into the drizzling rain. The watch overhear Borachio, his tongue liquor–loose, boast that he earned a thousand ducats for his villainy from Don John. Borachio then discourses upon fashion, calling it a deformed thief. Then he details how he wooed

Margaret, by the name of Hero, while being observed by Don John, Don Pedro, and Claudio from the orchard and how, believing the deceit, Claudio vowed to shame Hero at the wedding before the congregation the next day. The watch immediately takes them into custody.

Analysis

The tragic apprehensions stirred by the last scene are quickly relieved as Shakespeare introduces his broadly comic auxiliary plot in the person of the initimable Master Constable Dogberry, which brings a common touch to a play peopled with aristocrats. The scene is impeccably timed for the process of discovery and the direction of our dramatic responses and Dogberry's world of language parodies the syntactic landscapes of the other characters in the play and, as he says, "present[s] the Prince's own person."

As this prose scene opens, Dogberry instructs the watch with the zaniest misuse of language imaginable—"This is your charge: you shall comprehend all vagrom men," "[y]ou are thought here to be the most senseless and fit man for the constable of the watch," "for the watch to babble and talk is most tolerable and not to be endured," and "[b]e vitigant," all of which translates into normal police procedure—challenge suspicious characters, make no noise, send drunks home, don't strike too quickly and "let [a thief] show himself what he is and steal out of your company."

Dogberry is the name of a shrub that sprang up in every county of England, a commentary on the constabulatory of Shakespeare's day. The names Oatcake and Seacoal suggest that the men were dealers in these commodities and trained to read and write. The name Borachio is derived from a Spanish word meaning drunkard.

Seacoal follows Dogberry's instructions precisely and directs the watch to stand close as Borachio, "like a true drunkard, utter[s] all," which Shakespeare emphasizes by giving him plenty of sibilants to slur. Borachio brings the clothes imagery, sustained throughout the play, to a climactic point with his seemingly tangential discourse on fashion (116–42):

Borachio:	Thou knowest that the fashions of a doublet, or a hat, or a cloak is nothing to a man.
Conrade:	Yes, it is apparel.
Borachio:	Tush, I may as well say the fool's the fool. But seest thou not what a deformed thief this fashion is....Seest thou not, I say, what a deformed thief this fashion is, how giddily 'a turns about all the hot bloods between fourteen and five and thirty, sometimes fashioning them like Pharaoh's soldiers in the reechy painting, sometime like god Bel's priests in the old church window, sometime like the shaven Hercules in the smirched worm–eaten tapestry, where his codpiece seems as massy as his club?
Conrade:	All this I see and I see...that thou hast shifted out of thy tale into telling me of the fashion?
Borachio:	Not so either.

He finally gets to the meat of his story. Borachio, architect of this hoax, now repeatedly calls Don John his "master," claiming he made him do it:

	But know that I have tonight wooed Margaret, the Lady Hero's gentlewoman, by the name of Hero. She leans me out at her mistress' chamber window, bids me a thousand times good night—I tell this tale vilely; I should first tell thee how the Prince, Claudio and my master, planted and placed and possessed by my master Don John, saw afar off in the orchard this amiable encounter.
Conrade:	And thought they Margaret was Hero?
Borachio:	Two of them did, the Prince and Claudio, but the devil my master knew she was Margaret;

> and partly by his oaths, which first possessed
> them, partly by the dark night, which did
> deceive them, but chiefly by my villainy,
> which did confirm any slander that Don John
> had made, away went Claudio enraged;
> swore he would meet her, as he was ap-
> pointed, next morning at the temple, and
> there, before the congregation, shame her
> with what he saw o'ernight.

At this point, the watch charge him.

Shakespeare surprises us, placing the action of the deceit off–stage. There was no need to slow the action of his play, which, with all its play-acting and deception, has already called attention to its own devices of illusion. Instead, he moves the play forward by embellishing the discovery with a broadly comic brush.

Seacoal's recognition of one *Deformed*, is an allusion more popular in Shakespeare's time, but nonetheless funny. One *Deformed* may be a pun on a contemporary's name, possibly French, or a comment on the planet Uranus (in myth, a god maimed by his son, Cronus/Saturn), whose change of signs every seven years introduces an extreme change in fashion and public interest, called the *seven–year–itch* or a person born under that planet. The only thing we know for sure is that he wears a fashionable lock. Borachio's insistence that fashion, i.e., outer semblance, validly relates to his story of deception is a strong clue to the theme of the play.

We now know that Don John's plot will be revealed. Though fools, the watch is effective—they gather evidence before making an accusation, something their betters have not yet learned to do. Shakespeare maintains his comedic stance and prepares us for the scenes to follow by dissolving our tensions into hilarity.

Study Questions

1. Who gives the charge to the watch?

2. How does Dogberry instruct the watch to handle a thief?

3. What is the meaning of the phrase, "my elbow itched"?

4. In what manner does Borachio utter all to Conrade?

5. What does Borachio call a thief?

6. From where did Don John, Don Pedro, and Claudio witness Borachio wooing Margaret in Hero's name?

7. Who believed the staged deceit?

8. What did Claudio swear to do and why?

9. Who charges Borachio and Conrade?

10. How does the watch describe Borachio and Conrade?

Answers

1. Dogberry gives the charge to the watch.

2. Dogberry instructs the watch to, if they take a thief, let him show himself what he is and steal away out of your company.

3. "My elbow itched" is a proverbial warning against questionable companions.

4. Borachio, like a true drunkard, utters all to Conrade.

5. Borachio calls fashion a thief.

6. Don John, Don Pedro, and Claudio were in the orchard when they witnessed Borachio woo Margaret in Hero's name.

7. Don Pedro and Claudio believed the staged deceit.

8. Claudio, enraged, swore to disgrace Hero before the congregation the next morning at their wedding ceremony.

9. Seacoal charges Borachio and Conrade.

10. The watch describe Borachio and Conrade as "the most dangerous piece of lechery that ever was known in the commonwealth.

Suggested Essay Topics

1. Explain the comedic value of the watch. How do they move the action of the play forward? Why do you think they are

given to such outrageous misuse of language? Despite their lunacy, are they effective? Why?

2. Why did Conrade confess his villainy? Was it only the effect of liquor? Was there some other reason? If so, what was it? Why do you think so? Explain.

3. Shakespeare has placed the staged deceit off stage. Why? Is this effective? Explain.

Act III, Scene 4

Summary

The scene is set in the sitting room adjacent to Hero's bed-chamber. Hero sends Ursula to wake up Beatrice and tell her to come to the sitting room. Hero and Margaret discuss what she will wear. Beatrice arrives, sick, and tells Hero it is time to dress for the wedding. Margaret teasingly suggests to Beatrice that she take the herb, carduus benedictus, for her malady. Ursula returns to announce that the wedding party is ready to escort Hero to the church. The women hasten to the bed-chamber to dress her.

Analysis

This innocent prose scene, on the morning before the wedding, softens us to empathize with Hero. Margaret does not want Hero to wear a certain rebato, possibly the one she wore in the staged deceit the night before, but Hero lets us know she has a mind of her own by insisting on it, dismissing both Margaret and Beatrice as fools, and Margaret scandalizes Hero with her bawdy humor. This scene refreshes the fashion imagery and theme of outer appearance.

Beatrice's illness explains why she slept separately from Hero the night before; it also affords the ladies the opportunity to tease her about her new–found love. Margaret, fancying herself as good a wit as Beatrice, gets in a pointed stab when she advises Beatrice, "Get you some of this distilled carduus benedictus and lay it to your heart. It is the only thing for a qualm." And Hero quips, "There thou prick'st her with a thistle." The pun and double entendre is

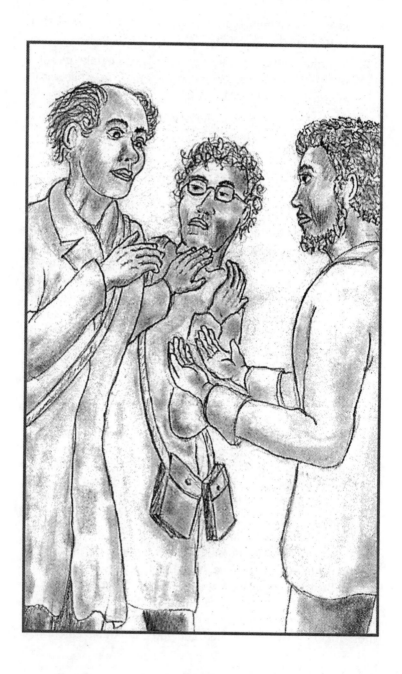

obvious. We, with the wedding party, await her as she runs off to dress.

Study Questions

1. Who does Hero send to wake up Beatrice?

2. What piece of clothing does Margaret try to talk Hero out of wearing?

3. Who does Hero call a fool?

4. Who is not feeling well?

5. Approximately what time is it?

6. What are Beatrice's symptoms?

7. Who attempts to wordspar with Beatrice in this scene?

8. What remedy does Margaret suggest for Beatrice's malady?

9. What is another name for benedictus?

10. What announcement does Ursula bring at the end of the scene?

Answers

1. Hero sends Ursula to wake up Beatrice.

2. Margaret tries to talk Hero out of wearing a specific rebato.

3. Hero calls both Margaret and her cousin, Beatrice, fools.

4. Beatrice is not feeling well.

5. It is approximately five o'clock.

6. Beatrice's symptoms are that she is stuffed and cannot smell.

7. Margaret attempts to wordspar with Beatrice in this scene.

8. Margaret suggests carduus benedictus as a remedy, lain on the heart.

9. Holy thistle is another name for benedictus.

10. Ursula announces that the wedding party has arrived to escort Hero to church.

Suggested Essay Topics

1. Why does Margaret wordspar with Beatrice? Would you say that she is somewhat imitative of Beatrice? How is her style, and her language different from Beatrice? Do you think she could ever win a match with Beatrice? Explain.

2. What is the purpose of this scene? How does it prepare us for the scene that is to follow? What tonal value does it have? Explain.

Act III, Scene 5

New Character:

Messenger: *calls Leonato to the wedding.*

Summary

The scene takes place in the hall in Leonato's house. Dogberry and Verges visit Leonato just as he is about to leave for the wedding. They chatter, trying Leonato's patience. Finally they tell him that they apprehended two suspicious characters who they want to have examined that morning before him. Leonato instructs them to take the examination and bring it to him. Leonato leaves to give Hero in marriage. Dogberry instructs Verges to send for Francis Seacoal, the sexton, to write down the examination which they will take at the jail.

Analysis

Shakespeare provides us with the most suspenseful moment of the play when Dogberry's tediousness and Leonato's impatience collide to prevent the disclosure of Don John's villainy before the wedding. Whatever the matter is, Leonato simply doesn't want to hear it. Ironically, he can't possibly imagine that anything these patronizing and tangential commoners could say would be of any interest to him. The dialogue is painfully funny:

Leonato:	Neighbors, you are tedious.
Dogberry:	It pleases your worship to say so, but we are the poor Duke's officers; but truly, for mine own part, if I were as tedious as a king, I could find in my heart to bestow it all of your worship.
Leonato:	All thy tediousness on me, ah?
Dogberry:	Yea, an 'twere a thousand pound more than 'tis; for I hear as good exclamation on your worship as of any man in the city, and though I be but a poor man, I am glad to hear it.
Leonato:	I would fain know what you have to say.

Verges then tells him they've taken prisoners, but Dogberry, not to be upstaged, pursues another loquacious tangent and an exasperated Leonato tells Dogberry to examine the prisoners himself. This is Dogberry's triumph and, fortunately, he will have only the best, learned writer take his first interrogation and so these men, "honest as the skin between their brows," who have done their job and "comprehend[ed] vagrom men," are off to the jail to question Borachio and Conrade. Knowing that, eventually, the wrong perpetrated against Hero will be righted, we proceed to the wedding.

Study Questions

1. Where does this scene take place?

2. Who visits Leonato in this scene?

3. Why doesn't Leonato listen to them carefully?

4. When Dogberry describes Verges' wits as not so blunt, what did he really mean?

5. What is Dogberry's response when Leonato tells him he is tedious?

6. What is Leonato's response when he finally understands that they have apprehended two people?

7. What hospitality does Leonato offer Dogberry and Verges before he leaves?

8. What message is brought to Leonato?

9. What direction does Dogberry give to Verges?

10. Why does Dogberry want a learned writer?

Answers

1. This scene takes place in the hall of Leonato's house.

2. Constable Dogberry and Headborough Verges visit Leonato.

3. Leonato doesn't listen to them carefully because he is distracted with the wedding, and in a hurry to get there.

4. Dogberry meant that Verges' wits were not so sharp.

5. Dogberry, upon being told that he is tedious, returns the compliment.

6. Leonato tells them to take the examination and to bring it to him.

7. Leonato offers wine to Dogberry and Verges.

8. The messenger tells Leonato that the wedding party is waiting for him to give his daughter in marriage.

9. Dogberry directs Verges to go to Francis Seacoal and bid him bring his pen and inkhorn to the jail.

10. Dogberry wants a learned writer to set down their excommunication (examination).

Suggested Essay Topics

1. How does this scene serve to move the action of the play forward? How necessary is it to the plot of the play? Would the play make any sense if this scene were cut out by a director? What would have happened to the action of the play if Leonato understood what Dogberry and Verges were talking about? Explain.

2. Why do Dogberry and Verges speak in such a tangential manner? What does their syntax tell you about their thinking processes? Do you think Leonato understood them at all? What did he understand? Cite the passages. If Leonato were not in a hurry to leave, would he have asked them to draw out the exact purpose of their visit? Explain.

Act IV

Act IV, Scene 1

New Characters:

Friar Francis: *priest at the nuptials of Claudio and Hero, who devises a plan to change the hearts of Claudio and Don Pedro and reverse the effects of the slander*

Attendants: *the bridal party*

Summary

This scene takes place before the altar in the church. Claudio contemptuously rejects Hero as a proved wanton. Leonato assumes that Claudio took Hero's virginity, which Claudio denies. Leonato appeals to the prince but Don Pedro, echoed by his brother, Don John, confirms Claudio's accusation. Claudio interrogates Hero about the man he saw at her window the night before. Hero denies the encounter. Claudio vows to love no more. Leonato seeks to be killed. Hero swoons. Don John, Don Pedro, and Claudio storm out of the church. Leonato, unable to believe that the two princes and Claudio could lie, accepts the slander as true and declares that if Hero is not dead he will kill her himself, disowning her. After Friar Francis recognizes her innocence and Benedick intuits that Don Pedro and Claudio have been misled by Don John, the good father directs Leonato to hide Hero away, to announce that she died upon being accused and to hold public mourning for her to change slander to remorse and to soften the heart of Claudio.

Beatrice and Benedick, suddenly alone before the altar, confess their love for one another. Benedick bids her to ask him to do anything for her. Beatrice answers with the chilling request, "[k]ill Claudio." Benedick asks Beatrice if she believes in her soul that Claudio wronged Hero. Receiving her affirmative answer, he agrees to challenge his friend and comrade-in-arms, Claudio.

Analysis

Shakespeare breaks the tone and movement of the comic action with a solemn ritual of marriage held before the altar, the visual effect of which is powerful and lends dignity to the scene. The first 21 lines of this scene are in prose, then in verse that ends in a quatrain (at 253) when the prose resumes.

Here we reach the climax of the many references to appearances and reality, when Claudio, locked in a world of sense evidence, in a church, before a congregation, accuses and refuses Hero, comparing her to a rotten orange. Dramatically, this crisis scene can be nothing but shocking, no matter how much we are prepared for it, and our mood is instantly altered.

Claudio, enjoying his revenge, takes his time to reject Hero and plays the injured lover to the hilt. He focuses his rejection on her name, asking her only one question (71–80):

Claudio:	Let me but move one question to your daughter; And by that fatherly and kindly power That you have in her, bid her answer truly.
Leonato:	I charge thee do so, as thou art my child.
Hero:	O, God defend me, how am I beset! What kind of catechizing call you this?
Claudio:	To make you answer truly to your name.
Hero:	Is it not Hero? Who can blot that name With any just reproach?

He can only justify his action with the words, "Are our eyes our own?" (71), echoed by Don Pedro, "Myself, my brother, and this grieved count/Did see her/Did hear her" (89–90). Then Claudio tearfully teeters in antithesis and pummels Hero with paradoxes (99–103):

> Oh Hero, what a Hero hadst thou been,
> If half thy outward graces had been placed
> About thy thoughts and counsels of they heart!
> But fare thee well, most foul, most fair! Farewell,
> Thou pure impiety and impious purity!

before storming out of the church, with a melodramatic vow never to love again, his immaturity revealed by his love for Hero's chaste image rather than her person.

When shocked Hero swoons, escaping into a coma, before an amazed congregation, her father, infected by the slander and burning with shame, falls into the cruel abyss of courtly code and seeks to regain his dignity with the death of his own daughter (120–127):

> Wherefore? Why doth not every earthly thing
> Cry shame upon her? Could she here deny
> The story that is printed in her blood?
> Do not live, Hero, do not ope thine eyes;
> For, did I think thou wouldst not quickly die,
> Thought I thy spirits were stronger than they shames,
> Myself would, on the rearward of reproaches,
> Strike at thy life.

He lapses into self–pity; he cannot believe the princes could lie. Only the friar, Benedick, and Beatrice show any concern for Hero, the real victim. Beatrice instantly recognizes Hero's innocence and her eight words, "O, on my soul my cousin is belied!," prepare us for the dialogue she will have with Benedick at the end of this scene.

The friar's innate wisdom and long experience in dealing with his flock gives him another point of view (155–170):

> Hear me a little;
> For I have only been silent so long
> And given way unto this course of fortune

By noting of the lady. I have marked
A thousand blushing apparitions
To start into her face, a thousand innocent shames
In angel whiteness beat away those blushes,
And in her eye there hath appeared a fire
To burn the errors that these princes hold
Against her maiden truth. Call me a fool;
Trust not my reading nor my observations,
Which with experimental seal doth warrant
The tenor of my book; trust not my age.
My reverance, calling, nor divinity,
If this sweet lady lie not guiltless here
Under some biting error.

Leonato cannot accept this readily since, holding to courtly code, he is ready to destroy whoever harmed him. Benedick astutely recognizes the error to be the practice of John, the Bastard. The benign hoax Father Francis suggests gives Leonato an immediate means of saving face and the experimental medicine he suggests for Claudio is guilt. We, the audience, look forward to seeing his remorse paraded before us.

The scene becomes poignant as everyone leaves the church except Benedick and Beatrice, still weeping for her cousin. The other characters have been exposed and we've been waiting for about a half-hour of playing time since Benedick and Beatrice recognized they were in love for this private moment. This is the climactic scene in the play when Benedick and Beatrice first confess their love for each other. Shakespeare used suspense and careful timing to bring us here and the rejection of Hero prepared us emotionally for its intimacy and intensity. Their crisis will counterpoint the one we have just witnessed and completely polarize the two plots. This is the point of greatest intensity in the play.

Benedick is the first to break through the wit–defended reserve that has kept them apart (267–272):

Benedick: I do love nothing in the world so well as you.
              Is not that strange?

| Beatrice: | As strange as the thing I know not. It were as possible for me to say I loved nothing so well as you. But believe me not; and yet I lie not. I confess nothing, nor I deny nothing. I am sorry for my cousin. |

He renews his avowal of love and Beatrice answers, "I love you with so much of my heart that none is left to protest." Then he makes his fatal error:

| Benedick: | Come, bid me do anything for thee. |
| Beatrice: | Kill Claudio. |

The comedic element of the play, subdued until this moment, momentarily pops back into place when Benedick, who offered to do anything that Beatrice wanted, refuses the very first thing she asks. But Beatrice cannot be happy in her love until her kinswoman is vindicated, and she displays the full depth and range of her emotional landscape to Benedick. In that context, this terse dialogue takes place:

| Benedick: | Think you in your soul the Count Claudio hath wronged Hero? |
| Beatrice: | Yea, as sure as I have a thought or a soul |

Benedick is engaged and leaves to seek out Claudio. He has passed his first test, which is to choose between his love for Beatrice and his friendship for Claudio.

Benedick and Beatrice's meeting, originally designed to furnish sport for their superficial friends, has occurred in a context of crisis and suffering. Their direct speech has reached the level of sincerity and they alone have resisted Don John's evil and agreed to vindicate Hero.

Study Questions

1. How does Claudio reject Hero?
2. What does Don Pedro call Hero?

3. What fate does Leonato wish upon his daughter, Hero, after she swoons away? And what extreme measure is he willing to take to bring it about?

4. Did Beatrice sleep with Hero the night before?

5. Who declares his belief that Hero is innocent?

6. Whom does Benedick intuit as the author of the slander?

7. What does Friar Francis direct Leonato to do?

8. For whom does Beatrice weep?

9. Who confess their love for each other?

10. Who will Benedick challenge?

Answers

1. Claudio rejects Hero contemptuously as a wanton.

2. Don Pedro calls Hero a common stale.

3. Leonato wishes his daughter dead and he is willing to kill her himself.

4. No, Beatrice did not sleep with Hero the night before.

5. Friar Francis declares his belief that Hero is innocent.

6. Benedick intuits Don John as the author of the slander.

7. Friar Francis directs Leonato to hide Hero away, to announce that she died upon being accused, and to hold public mourning for her.

8. Beatrice weeps for her cousin, Hero.

9. Beatrice and Benedict confess their love for each other.

10. Benedick will challenge his friend, Claudio.

Suggested Essay Topics

1. Claudio and Don Pedro have publicly shamed Hero. Discuss the impact of this serious action on Hero and her kinsmen. Do you think they will ever forgive Claudio and Don Pedro? Cite specific dialogue from the text to support your position.

2. How does Leonato respond to the slander? What does his response tell you about his character? Why is he so easily swayed by the opinions of others? What do you suppose his next action will be? Why?

3. What is the wisdom of the priest? What faculty does he employ to see Hero's innocence. What kind of knowledge is the basis of his plan? Do you think his strategy will work? Cite the text to explain.

4. What moves Benedick to challenge Claudio? Do you think that Beatrice was right to ask him to kill Claudio? Defend your position.

Act IV, Scene 2

New Character:

Sexton (Francis Seacoal): *town clerk, a learned writer who, taking down the examination of Borachio and Conrade, recognizes the importance of its contents and immediately delivers it to Leonato*

Summary

This scene takes place at the jail. Dogberry, under the direction of the sexton, examines Borachio and Conrade. Speaking directly into Borachio's ear, Dogberry accuses him and Conrade of false knavery, which Borachio denies. The first watch and Seacoal testify that they heard Borachio confess to receiving a thousand ducats from Don John for slandering Hero. The sexton announces that Don John fled after Hero was accused and refused and that Hero, upon the grief of this, suddenly died. He directs the constable to bind the men and bring them to Leonato's and leaves immediately to show the examination to the governor. About to be bound, Conrade calls Dogberry an ass. Scandalized, Dogberry wants all to remember that he is an ass, although it will not be written down.

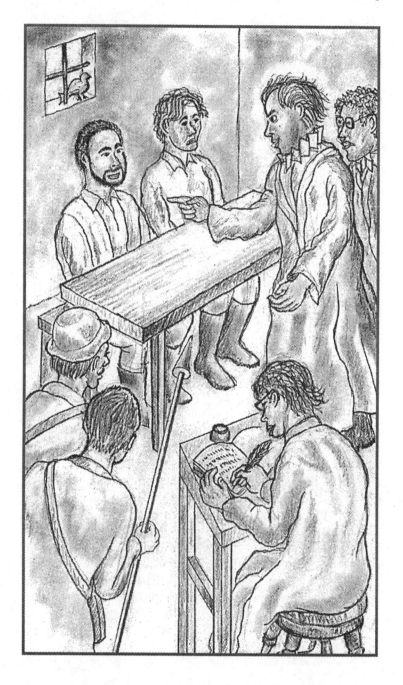

Analysis

It is part of Shakespeare's genius to let the action of this play begin its fall with a new comic vision. Considered one of "the funniest scenes ever written" (Joseph Papp), this is where the final block of the play's action, which will resolve the polarized plots, begins.

Dogberry's opening line is, "Is our whole dissembly appeared?" We can imagine that he wears his very best judicial gown. Formal, saturnine, Conrade is immediately annoyed by him, presumably for being addressed as "sirrah", a contemptuous extension of sire, used to address inferiors. Dogberry's swearing–in ceremony would panic any lawyer:

Dogberry:	Masters, do you serve God?
Conrade:	Borachio. Yea sir, we hope.
Dogberry:	Write down that they hope they serve God; and write God first, for God should go before such villains!

Fortunately, the sexton understands judicial procedure and moves the examination along by having the watch called as the accusers. This doesn't stop Dogberry's tangents and he keeps close watch that each word elicited is written down. As he hears the testimony of Seacoal, seemingly for the first time (which would explain why he didn't know the importance of his prisoners when he spoke to Leonato), he tells the villains, "Thou wilt be condemned into everlasting redemption for this." The sexton confirms the events the watch testified to and leaves immediately to bring the examination to Leonato. Timing is still important to the action and Leonato must be prepared to move promptly.

As Dogberry is about "to opinion" them (translation: tie up), Conrade calls him a coxcomb and he is shocked at this stab to his office. But when Conrade calls him an ass, our petit bourgeois clown is beside himself, and his world of big words collapses (74–86):

I am a wise fellow, and, which is more, an officer;
and, which is more, a householder; and, which is

more, as pretty a piece of flesh as any is in
Messina; and one that knows the law, go to; and a
rich fellow enough, go to; and a fellow that hath
had losses; and one that hath two gowns and
everything handsome about him. Bring him away.
O, that I had been writ down an ass!

He parodies the "much ado" of the other characters in his self–
important concern for the outward trappings of status and in his
inability to grasp a clear thought.

Study Questions

1. Who is provided with a stool and a cushion?

2. Is Dogberry's examination of the prisoners direct and to the point?

3. Who moves the examination along and keeps it on point?

4. What does Dogberry whisper into Borachio's ear?

5. What is the testimony of the watch?

6. What is Dogberry's response upon hearing the watch testify that Count Claudio intended to accuse and refuse Hero?

7. Who confirms the testimony of the watch?

8. Who leaves to show Leonato the examination?

9. Does the news of Hero's death upon wrongful accusation have any effect on Conrade?

10. What does Dogberry want everyone to remember?

Answers

1. The sexton is provided with a stool and a cushion.

2. No. Dogberry's examination is extremely tangential and practically pointless.

3. The sexton moves the examination along and keeps it on point.

4. Dogberry whispers into Borachio's ear that "it is thought that you are false knaves."

5. The watch testifies that they heard Borachio call Don John a villain, who paid him a thousand ducats for slandering Hero and state that Count Claudio would disgrace and refuse Hero.

6. Upon hearing of Count Claudio's intention to accuse and refuse Hero, Dogberry tells Borachio that he will "be condemned into everlasting redemption for this."

7. The sexton confirms the testimony of the watch.

8. The sexton leaves to show Leonato the examination.

9. The news of Hero's death upon wrongful accusation has no effect on Conrade. On the contrary, it sobers him not at all, and he calls Dogberry an ass.

10. Dogberry wants everyone to remember that he is an ass.

Suggested Essay Topics

1. Why did Shakespeare put this broad comic scene directly after the crisis? What effect does this have on the audience? In what way does it move the action of the play forward? Explain.

2. Do you think this is the first time that Dogberry has examined a prisoner? Why is Dogberry unable to keep to the point? What is his mind preoccupied with? What would this examination have been like, had the sexton not intervened? What is Shakespeare telling us about the constabulatory of his time and their use of the legal system?

3. What prompts Conrade to call Dogberry an ass? Why does Dogberry perserve about being called an ass? Is he an ass? Cite passages from the text to defend your position.

SECTION SIX

Act V

Act V, Scene 1

Summary

The scene takes place in the street before the house of Leonato. Antonio tries to philosophize his brother, Leonato, out of his grief. Leonato says that his passion cannot be patched with proverbs and bids him to cease his counsel. Antonio advises him to make those who have harmed him suffer also, and Leonato vows to defend Hero's honor. At this point Claudio and Don Pedro cross their path. Both Leonato and Antonio challenge Claudio for the villainy of slandering Hero to death. Don Pedro tells them the charge against Hero was full of proof and refuses to listen further. Vowing that he will be heard, Leonato exits with his brother just as Benedick arrives.

Claudio and Don Pedro seek Benedick's wit to lift their spirits. Benedick challenges Claudio. Taking it as a jest, both Claudio and Don Pedro seek to enjoy their usual banter. Benedick tells Don Pedro that he must discontinue his company and repeats his challenge to Claudio. He informs them that Don John has fled Messina and that they killed an innocent lady. As Benedick exits, they realize that he is earnest. Don Pedro, in growing awareness, notes that his brother has fled.

The constables and the watch enter with Borachio and Conrade. Don Pedro recognizes them as his brother's men and asks Dogberry the nature of their offense. Finding Dogberry's answer too oblique to be understood, he questions Borachio. Borachio asks

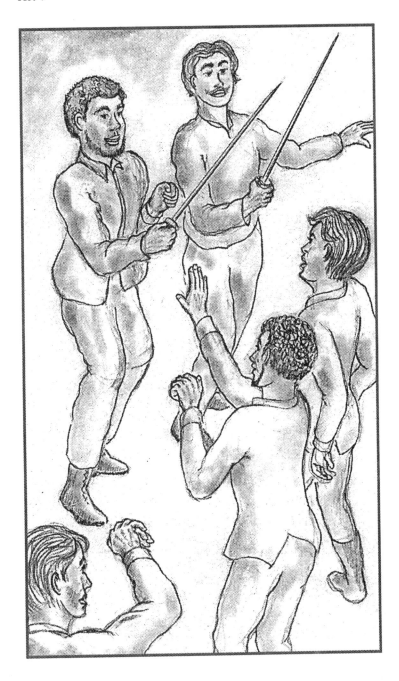

Don Pedro to let Count Claudio kill him and tells him that the watch overheard him confess his paid collusion in Don John's slander of Hero. Claudio now sees Hero in the light of the innocence he first loved her for.

Leonato and Antonio return with the sexton. Borachio declares sole responsibility for the death of Hero, but Leonato tells him that Don John, Don Pedro, and Claudio had a hand in it. Both Claudio and Don Pedro ask for a penance, claiming mistaking as their only sin. As penance, Leonato assigns them both the task of publicly mourning Hero and declaring her innocence. He assigns Claudio the further task of accepting his niece, sight unseen, in marriage the next morning. Dogberry takes this opportunity to tell Leonato that Conrade called him an ass and that the watch overheard the prisoners talk of another knave, one *Deformed*. Leonato thanks the watch and tips Dogberry. A thankful Dogberry humbly gives him leave to depart. As they leave, Don Pedro and Claudio promise to perform their penance. Leonato instructs the watch to bring the prisoners, then departs to question Margaret about her acquaintance with Borachio.

Analysis

Throughout the play Shakespeare has kept us informed of the truth while his characters deceive each other (at this point the sexton is on his way to Leonato's and Hero is not dead), which puts us into a somewhat removed orientation that increases the comic value of the action. In a sense, he has manipulated us into believing we're above it all. This scene opens with a grief–stricken but wordy Leonato, speaking in verse. Were his dialogue in a tragedy, we might be teary, but knowing that he will soon have proof that his daughter was slandered we are unlikely to extend him much sympathy, which tones down his indignation to a subtly comic level. Leonato refuses to be consoled by Antonio, dismissing him with (35–37):

> I pray thee, peace. I will be flesh and blood;
> For there was never yet philosopher
> That could endure the toothache patiently.

This echoes Benedick's toothache speech in Act III. He will take Antonio's suggestion to seek revenge, and he gets his opportunity immediately as Don Pedro and Claudio enter. The comedy leaps forward as Antonio flaunts his courage as he joins Leonato in challenging the young swordsman, knowing full well that neither Claudio nor the prince can dishonor themselves by fighting men of their advanced age. Don Pedro breaks up the mock challenge by saying a sympathetic word to Leonato, but when Don Pedro turns a cold ear to Leonato's appeal, he leaves, determined to be heard. His brother, Antonio, gives the exit a comic flourish by insinuating another challenge to come, a kind of or else. We, the audience, know all will be reconciled when Dogberry arrives. Note the dialogue change to prose at line 110, which continues until Dogberry's entrance, when it changes to a mixture of verse and prose.

Benedick enters and we know his mind; he is in his steely fighting mode. But his friends, Claudio and Don Pedro, who were seeking out his wit to lift their exhausted spirits (isolated by the renunciation) when they came across Leonato, don't get it. They take Benedick's dignified and sober expression as a joke, a masquerade to amuse them. This forces Benedick's attempts to deliver the challenge to Claudio to escalate the comedy somewhat as he takes him aside to deliver it. Claudio hears it but again doesn't understand it, and Don Pedro attempts to rag him about Beatrice. Benedick, void of levity, is firm and gentlemanly as he departs (185–190):

> My Lord, for your many courtesies I thank you. I
> must discontinue your company. Your brother the
> bastard is fled from Messina. You have among you
> killed a sweet and innocent lady. For my Lord
> Lackbeard there, he and I shall meet, and till then
> peace be with him.

Now they know that he is earnest. And Don Pedro, in growing awareness, says, "Did he not say my brother was fled?" which is the cue for Dogberry's entrance.

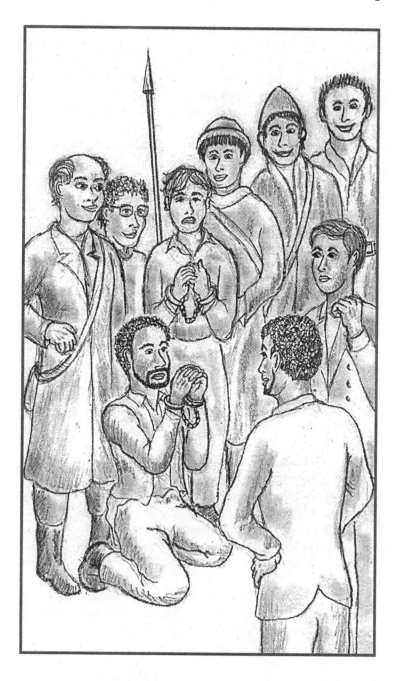

The theatrical spectacle of Dogberry and Verges parading their bound prisoners, secured by the watch, will get their attention, and Don Pedro immediately recognizes his brother's men. Of course, we know what is likely to happen when he inquires after their offense, and Dogberry does not disappoint us (211-215):

> Marry, sir, they have committed false report;
> moreover, they have spoken untruths; second-
> arily, they are slanders; sixth and lastly, they have
> belied a lady; thirdly, they have verified unjust
> things; and to conclude, they are lying knaves.

The obliqueness of his answer allows them a short interlude of amusement until they find out the truth from Borachio (227-234):

> What your wisdoms could not discover, these
> shallow fools have brought to light, who in the
> night overheard me confessing to this man how
> Don John your brother incensed me to slander the
> Lady Hero, how you were brought into the orchard
> and saw me court Margaret in Hero's garments,
> how you disgraced her when you should marry her.

There is an immediate tonal change. That Borachio was so converted by news of Hero's death implies that his drunken confession in Act III was a move in conscience. Friar Francis' curative has taken hold and to Claudio's eyes returns the pristine image of the Hero he wanted to marry. Claudio owns the sin of mistaking (sin means error, mistake, wander or stray, and in Hebrew means muddy). Dogberry reminds his men to specify that he is an ass. The scene, from Borachio's statement to this point reflects the passage of St. Paul in *I Corinthians*, 1:27–28:

> God hath chosen the foolish things of the world
> to confound the wise; and God hath chosen the
> weak things of the world to confound the things
> which are mighty; and base things of the world

and things which are despised, hath God chosen,
yea, and things which are not, to bring to nought
things that are.

This may be the source for the invention of the constable and
his watch. Certainly, Dogberry's discovery is purely providential,
perhaps the answer to Friar Francis' prayer.

Now Shakespeare brings Leonato and Antonio back, and full
of dignity, Leonato asks, "[w]hich is the villain?" When Borachio
comes forth to claim full responsibility, Leonato, as he promised
in his exit earlier in the scene, is heard (259–264):

No, not so, villain, thou beliest thyself.
Here stand a pair of honorable men—
A third is fled—that had a hand in it.
I thank you, princes, for my daughter's death.
Record it with your high and worthy deeds.
'Twas bravely done, if you bethink you of it.

Claudio is instantly positioned to ask for a penance, echoed by Don
Pedro. Leonato's wisdom, which he must have to be in the position of governor now shows through as he assigns the comic penance of hanging up verses at the empty tomb in a public mourning
and the practical penance of clearing Hero's name. But the real test
of Claudio's repentance is his willingness to marry Leonato's fic-
tional niece, sight unseen.

Borachio's vindication of Margaret is necessary to keep the
action from swerving out of its steady course to the resolution. This
is Dogberry's opportunity to tag on his tangential thoughts with:
(299–302):

[m]oreover, sir, which indeed is not under white
 and black, this plaintiff here, the offender, did call
 me an ass. I beseech you, let it be remembered in
 his punishment.

He goes on to share his concern with another *vagrom*, one
Deformed, about whom he has apparently gathered an extended

dossier, again parodying the much ado of the play's plot structure which was just as unreal, before saying adieu to Leonato:

> I humbly give you leave to depart; and if a merry
> meeting be wished, God prohibit it!

Study Questions

1. What kind of philosopher does Leonato say never existed?

2. Which characters challenge Claudio?

3. What is Benedick's reply when asked by Claudio if he will use his wit?

4. What does Benedick tell Claudio and Don Pedro about Don John?

5. What does Borachio tell Don Pedro about the watch?

6. Does Leonato accept Borachio's claim to be solely responsible for Hero's death?

7. Does Borachio name Margaret as a co–conspirator in the slander of Hero?

8. What penance does Leonato give to Claudio and Don Pedro?

9. What does Dogberry want Leonato to remember when punishing Conrade?

10. Whom will Leonato talk with and why?

Answers

1. Leonato says, "[t]here was never yet a philosopher that could endure the toothache patiently."

2. Claudio is challenged by Leonato, by Antonio, and by Benedick.

3. Benedick replies, "It is in my scabbard. Shall I draw it?"

4. Benedick tells Claudio and Don Pedro that Don John has fled Messina.

5. Borachio tells Don Pedro "[w]hat your wisdoms could not discover, these shallow fools have brought to light."

6. No. Leonato tells Borachio that Don Pedro, Claudio, and Don John had a hand in it.

7. No. Borachio declares Margaret innocent of any conspiracy in the slander of Hero.

8. As penance, Leonato assigns them the task of informing Messina of Hero's innocence. Claudio will hang an epitaph upon her tomb, sing it to her bones that evening, and marry his niece, sight unseen, the next morning.

9. Dogberry wants Leonato to remember, when punishing Conrade, that he called him an ass.

10. Leonato will talk with Margaret to find out how her acquaintance grew with Borachio.

Suggested Essay Topics

1. Why do Don Pedro and Claudio seek Benedick to cheer them? Does their jocularity seem strange in light of the fact that they know Hero is dead? Why did they assume that Benedick was jesting? What did it take to sober them to the point of feeling anything for Leonato and Hero? What are they willing to own up to? What does this tell you about their characters? Use their dialogue to explain.

2. Borachio wishes to be killed for his villainy. Does this surprise you? Why does he protect Margaret and claim sole responsibility for killing Hero? What do these acts tell you about his character, and how did the action of the drama affect him? Interpret and explain.

3. For the penance requested by Claudio and Don Pedro, Leonato assigns them both the task of publicly mourning Hero and declaring her innocence. He assigns Claudio the further task of accepting his niece, sight unseen, in marriage. What wisdom does Leonato show in the assignment? Is it fair? What effect do you expect the performed penance to have on Claudio, Don Pedro, and the public? Give a detailed explanation.

Act V, Scene 2

Summary

Benedick and Margaret meet outside Leonato's house. He bids her to call Beatrice to him and unsuccessfully attempts a sonnet. Beatrice complies with his request immediately. When Benedick toyfully marks (notes) that she comes when bidden, she bids him to tell her what has passed between he and Claudio. Benedick reports that Claudio undergoes his challenge. A witty interchange ensues as each seeks the other to tell the virtues for which they are loved and concludes with Benedick's declaration that they are "too wise to woo peaceably." Ursula appears to call them to Leonato's, with the news that Hero has been cleared, Don Pedro and Claudio were absolved, and Don John declared the villain.

Analysis

The double entendres between Benedick and Margaret that open this short prose scene serve to entertain us. This charming scene is technically important as part of the falling action of the play and prepares us for its solution and denouement as we await the findings of Leonato's judicial examination. This is Benedick's first breath of air since the chapel scene earlier in the morning, and his first opportunity to bask in the knowledge that his love for Beatrice is requited. He sings, no matter how pitifully, William Elderton's ditty, "The God of love/That sits above/And knows me/And knows me," which is sure to draw a chuckle from the audience as he attempts sonnet-writing and concludes (30–41):

> in loving, Leander the good swimmer, Troilus the
> first employer of panders, and a whole bookful of
> these quondam carpetmongers, whose names yet
> run smoothly in the even road of a blank verse,
> why, they were never so truly turned over and over
> as my poor self in love.... No, I was not born under
> a rhyming planet, nor I cannot woo in festival terms.

Beatrice's entrance saves him from the attempt. His short experiment with institutionalized romance completed, he will love Beatrice honestly and in his own way.

It is obvious that he is more interested in wooing Beatrice than talking about his challenge to Claudio. As their good–natured dialogue continues in explorations of nimble wit, Benedick observes, "Thou and I are too wise to woo peaceably."

Study Questions

1. Who does Benedick meet at the opening of the scene?
2. Was Benedict born under a rhyming planet?
3. Does Beatrice come when she is called by Benedick?
4. What news did Beatrice want to find out?
5. What does Benedick tell Beatrice about Claudio?
6. For which of Benedick's bad parts did Beatrice first fall in love with him?
7. Why does Benedick suffer love for Beatrice?
8. Why can't Benedick and Beatrice woo peaceably?
9. Who is Don Worm?
10. What news does Ursula bring?

Answers

1. Benedick meets Margaret at the opening of the scene.
2. Benedick was not born under a rhyming planet.
3. Beatrice comes when she is called by Benedick.
4. Beatrice wanted to find out if Benedick challenged Claudio.
5. Benedick tells Beatrice that Claudio undergoes his challenge.
6. Beatrice first fell in love with Benedick for all of his bad parts.
7. Benedick suffers love for Beatrice because he loves her against his will.
8. Benedick and Beatrice are too wise to woo peaceably.
9. Don Worm is the action of the conscience, traditionally described as the gnawing of a worm.
10. Ursula brings the news that "It has been proved my Lady

Hero hath been falsely accused, the Prince and Claudio mightily abused, and Don John is the author of all, who is fled and gone."

Suggested Essay Topics

1. What does Benedick mean when he tells us he was not born under a rhyming planet? What does he mean when he says he cannot woo in festival terms? Does this mean he is a bad lover? How do you think he will love Beatrice? Explain.

2. Benedick tells Beatrice that they are too wise to woo peaceably. Is this true? Do you think less wise people woo any more peaceably than they do? Explain, citing examples from the text.

Act V, Scene 3

Summary

Claudio and Don Pedro, accompanied by a party of lords and musicians, arrive at the monument of Leonato to perform a public mourning for Hero. Claudio reads an epitaph which declares her innocence and then hangs it up at her tomb. Balthasar sings a hymn to Diana, patroness of chastity, entreating her to forgive Hero's slanderers. Claudio vows to do the rite yearly. At dawn the mourners leave, each going their separate way. Claudio and Don Pedro will change their garments and go to Leonato's for the wedding.

Analysis

The redemption scene, with its epitaph, song, and dialogue, is wholly in rhyme with the exception of the first two lines. At midnight our penitents arrive at Leonato's monument and withdraw into a world of contrition as they enter the damp tomb to experience the spiritual medicine of Friar Francis' restorative, accompanied by a silent black-robed procession with flickering tapers.

Claudio reads the epitaph to Hero, "done to death by slanderous tongues," that he has written (which requires deep-felt delivery to work), hangs up the scroll for public scrutiny, and calls for the dirge (12–21):

> Pardon, goddess of the night,
> Those that slew thy virgin knight;
> For the which, with songs of woe,
> Round about her tomb they go.
> Midnight, assist our moan;
> Help us to sigh and groan,
> Heavily, heavily.
> Graves, yawn and yield your dead,
> Till death be uttered,
> Heavily, heavily.

While it is sung the mourners circle the tomb. The tone is solemn. They beg pardon of Diana, moon goddess and patroness of chastity, and invoke midnight and the shades of the dead to assist them as they proclaim Hero's innocent death.

This scene carries an other-worldly quality and its comic element is subdued almost entirely, asking for no more than a knowing chuckle. We are convinced that Friar Francis' nostrum has taken hold when Claudio volunteers to perform the ceremony yearly, until his death, and his reformation prepares the audience to accept him as a worthy husband for Hero.

Study Questions

1. Where does the action take place?

2. What is the action?

3. Who reads the epitaph to Hero?

4. After reading the epitaph, what does Claudio do with the scroll?

5. Who sings the hymn to Hero?

6. Who is the goddess of the night?

7. How often does Claudio vow to perform this rite?

8. At what time of day do they end their rite?

9. Who dismisses the mourning company?

10. What will Claudio and Don Pedro do next?

Answers

1. The action takes place at the tomb of Hero, in the monument of Leonato.

2. The action is a public rite of mourning.

3. Claudio reads the epitaph to Hero.

4. After reading the epitaph, Claudio hangs up the scroll.

5. Balthasar sings the hymn to Hero.

6. Diana, the moon goddess and patroness of chastity, is the goddess of the night.

7. Claudio vows to do this rite yearly.

8. They end their rite at dawn.

9. Don Pedro dismisses the mourning company.

10. Claudio and Don Pedro will change their clothes and proceed to Leonato's.

Suggested Essay Topics

1. Claudio vows to perform this rite of mourning to Hero yearly. Does this vow indicate a change in consciousness? Explain the rite of passage Claudio has gone through while performing his penance, detailing each inner action of conscience as you see it in your mind's eye.

2. Why does Shakespeare place this action during the night in a tomb, lit only by candles, and end it at the break of dawn? What does this symbolize? What theatrical effect does this have on the audience? Would this scene, though a public mourning, have worked as well in full sunlight? Explain.

Act V, Scene 4

Summary

This scene takes place in the hall in Leonato's house. Musicians are seated in the gallery. Hero, the prince, and Claudio have been declared innocent, and Margaret in some fault for the slander. Benedick is relieved that he need no longer keep Claudio under his challenge. Leonato directs Hero and the other ladies to withdraw and return, masked, when he sends for them. He directs Antonio to play the father of the bride. When Benedick asks Leonato for Beatrice's hand in marriage and Leonato exposes the double gull, Benedick, though nonplussed at Leonato's answer, reaffirms his request and receives Leonato's blessing.

Prince Don Pedro and Claudio arrive with attendants. Claudio answers in the affirmative when asked by Leonato if he will marry his niece. While Antonio summons Hero and the ladies, Claudio attempts to tease Benedick. Benedick briskly dismisses Claudio with an insult to his heritage. Antonio returns with Hero and the ladies, who are masked. Claudio swears before the friar that he will marry Antonio's masked daughter. When Hero lifts her veil, he and Don Pedro are amazed. Leonato explains that she was dead only as long as her slander lived, which the friar promises to explain. Benedick asks the friar which of the ladies is Beatrice. Unmasking, she coyly steps forth from the line of women. Benedick asks Beatrice if she loves him and she responds "no more than reason," which he echoes, and when Beatrice asks Benedick if he loves her, they both detail the particulars of their separate gulls, at which point Claudio and Hero step forth with papers, written in their hands, which evidence their love for each other. Benedick stops the wordplay with a kiss. When Don Pedro attempts to mock Benedick as a married man, Benedick refuses the bait and declares that since he purposes to marry he will not entertain any thing against it, including his own past parodies of the state. Claudio and Benedick resume their friendship. Benedick spiritedly calls for music and dance to lighten their hearts and advises the matchmaker, Don Pedro, to "[g]et thee a wife, get thee a wife." A messenger arrives with news that Don John has been taken, and is being

brought back to Messina. The play ends with Benedick's call to the pipers and an exuberant dance.

Analysis

In the denouement and resolution of the play, Shakespeare ties its loose ends up amiably, rejoining the polarized plots with a reconciliation scene. He clearly indicates he will do this in Friar Francis' dialogue, "Well I'm glad all things sorts so well." He immediately tells us that the prince and Claudio have been absolved, that Margaret underwent Leonato's examination and escaped with slight censure, and that Benedick has released Claudio from his challenge. The first 90 lines of this scene are in verse, including speeches by Benedick and Beatrice, and the rest is in prose except for the messenger's two verse lines interjected at its end.

Leonato's confession of the double gull does not sway Benedick from his determination to marry Beatrice. Although he tells Leonato that his answer is "enigmatical," it is unlikely that anyone as alert as Benedick does not understand his meaning, and his comical remark serves not only to end any exploration of the matter at this time and to affirm his commitment, but also serves to advise us that Benedick has reached a new level of self-acceptance.

Both Leonato and Benedick continue their reserve with Don Pedro and Claudio until the penance is fulfilled and their dialogue is direct, shorn of ornamentation. Benedick ignores the prince's gibe about his "February face" and disposes of Claudio's crude rally with caustic severity. Claudio's insensitivity (basically a play for masculine approval and probably developed during the war), though he is well–bred, indicates the immaturity which caught him in the circumstances of the play to begin with. The inappropriateness of his remarks serve to maintain a comic element to counterpoint the other characters' reserve. Without it, the denouement of the play would flatten.

Claudio, having submitted all choice to Leonato, has mourned at the tomb and, having rejected Hero on the basis of outer appearance (hubris), must now prove himself by accepting Leonato's masked niece as his wife (nemesis). His submission assures Leonato that there will be no similar trouble in the family in the future. It is here that Shakespeare puts his greatest emphasis on the mask motif and the row of masked ladies both parallel and counterpoint the masquerade ball in Act II, in which the men wore the masks.

Hero lifts her veil, after Claudio vowed before the holy friar to marry her, and we see an amazed Claudio. The benign hoax had such a salutary effect that his contrition makes it hard for him to believe that she is alive. Reunited with the reborn Hero, he is readily forgiven, in the Christian tradition, for, after all, the wrong done to Hero was not a betrayal of love and trust but an assault on her reputation and the break–off of a desirable marriage—wrongs easily righted. The decorous dialogue, so elaborate in the exposition, is now pared to the bone, void of polite routine. All oblique references are gone, and any question promises a prompt answer. At this point, the Claudio-Hero plot is resolved as the giving of trust and the move toward faith. The suspense has ended; they will be married.

Our three–dimensional players, Benedick and Beatrice, complete their journey that began as a trial of verbal supremacy, developed as the ability to see themselves as part of the human comedy rather than clever onlookers, and now concludes with the spontaneous and loving expression of their combined, generous wit. Their dialogue has lost none of its vitality and now expresses itself in unchecked joy and merriment that springs from their new levels of inner awareness.

Beatrice continues to keep Benedick wondering by playfully hiding herself among the masked ladies, secure in the knowledge that he will seek her out, and steps forward coyly when he asks where she is. They gracefully face the truth about their courtship publicly in an articulate exchange which is the exact antithesis that matchmaker Don Pedro had looked forward to:

> The sport will be when they hold one an opinion
> of another's dotage, and no such matter; that's the
> scene I would like to see, which will be merely a
> dumb show.

A renewed Benedick will be no man's fool when it comes to the subject of love, and he responds to Don Pedro's baiting question, "[h]ow dost thou, Benedick, the married man?" with:

> I'll tell thee what, Prince: a college of witcrackers
> cannot flout me out of my humor. Dost thou think
> I care for a satire or an epigram? No. If a man will
> be beaten with brains, 'a shall wear nothing hand-
> some about him. In brief, since I do purpose to
> marry, I will think nothing to any purpose that the world
> can say against it; and therefore never flout
> at me for what I have said against it; for man is a
> giddy thing, and this is my conclusion.

So ends the fashion metaphor. Benedick is saying that a slave to convention will never be true to himself; that if he lives in fear of an epigram, he dare not marry a beautiful woman. He responds to Claudio's macho baiting by declaring his friendship for him. All defenses collapsed, Benedick insists on celebrating with music and dance and tells Don Pedro, the matchmaker, to "get thee a wife, get thee a wife."

This ends the play. Shakespeare has completed the three phases of his play: recognition of love, stress of trial, and resolution with love's confirmation. The lesson the play teaches is to learn to discriminate properly and to estimate everything at its true value. In the end, the counterplots initiated by the two princes have brought only the good result of strengthening love. Perhaps Shakespeare is saying that all of us, as Claudio claims, sin only through "mistaking".

It is not surprising that this is the only play of Shakespeare that ends with a dance because a play of such musicality as *Much Ado About Nothing* can only end with a dance—an exuberant dance! We have taken the emotional journey with the players, and re-newed, we go our separate ways.

Study Questions

1. Who is declared innocent?

2. When Benedick asks Leonato for Beatrice's hand and Leonato reveals the double gull, what is Benedick's response?

3. Who is the masked lady that Claudio swore to marry and how does he respond when she unveils herself?

4. What paper does Claudio produce?

5. How does Benedick stop Beatrice's mouth?

6. What is Benedick's conclusion?

7. Who wants to dance and why?

8. What advice does Benedick give Don Pedro?

9. What news does the messenger bring?

10. Which plays of Shakespeare end with a dance?

Answers

1. Hero, the prince, and Claudio are declared innocent.

2. Benedick's response is, "[y]our answer, sir, is enigmatical."

3. Claudio is amazed to find the masked lady that he swore to marry is none other than Hero.

4. Claudio produces a paper containing a halting sonnet written by Benedick.

5. Benedick stops Beatrice's mouth with a kiss.

6. Benedick's conclusion is "man is a giddy thing."

7. Benedick wants to dance to lighten their hearts and their wive's heels.

8. Benedick advises Don Pedro to "[g]et thee a wife, get thee a wife."

9. The messenger brings the news that Don John is taken and will be brought back to Messina.

10. No other plays of Shakespeare end with a dance.

Suggested Essay Topics

1. Why does Hero readily forgive Claudio for accusing and re-
    fusing her? Do you think this is a typical reaction? What do
    you think their marriage will be like? Explain.

2. As Benedick's values change during the play, so do his musi-
    cal allusions. In this scene, it is Benedick who wants music,
    and specifically, pipers—even before the wedding! What does
    this indicate to you? Citing specific passages, compare this
    scene with his previous responses to music and discuss how
    they indicate his growing response to love.

3. Benedick tells Prince Don Pedro, the matchmaker, to get
    himself a wife. What kind of wife would he require? Would
    he invite his brother, Don John, to the wedding? Do you think
    he is ready for marriage? Why? Explain.

SECTION SEVEN

Sample Analytical Paper Topics

The following paper topics, each with a sample outline, are designed to test your understanding of *Much Ado About Nothing*. Each deals with the play as a whole and requires analysis of important themes and literary devices.

Topic #1

Shakespeare interweaves two love stories in *Much Ado About Nothing*, the Claudio–Hero plot and the Benedick–Beatrice plot. Write an analytical essay on the ways in which they parallel or counterpoint each other in characterization, in dialogue, and in plot structure.

Outline

I.   Thesis Statement: *The Claudio–Hero and the Benedick–Beatrice love stories are interwoven in* Much Ado About Nothing *through a series of parallels and contrasts in characterization, in dialogue, and in plot structure.*

II. Characterization

    A.   Parallels

        1.   Hero and Beatrice are kinswomen and good friends and Claudio and Benedick are comrades–in–arms and good friends

2. Both couples knew each other in the past

3. Both couples are learning to discriminate properly and to estimate each other's true value

4. Both couples' ability to love will be tested

B. Contrasts

1. Claudio and Hero are slaves to convention and Benedick and Beatrice are free spirits

2. Claudio seeks a wooing intermediary and Benedick woos directly

3. Claudio and Hero rely on knowledge, and Benedick and Beatrice rely on their intuition.

4. After professing their love, Claudio and Hero are easily derailed, but nothing will stop Benedick and Beatrice

III. Dialogue

A. Parallels

1. Both couples are educated aristocrats

2. Both couples talk about marriage

3. Both Claudio and Benedick speak about their fears of cuckoldry

4. Both couples will learn to speak more directly

B. Contrasts

1. Claudio and Hero usually speak in verse and Benedick and Beatrice usually speak in prose

2. Claudio and Hero comply with social superior's voices and Benedick and Beatrice challenge social superior's voices

3. Benedick and Beatrice radically change their speech patterns and Claudio and Hero do not

IV. Plot structure

A. Harmony of plots

    1. The Claudio–Hero plot and the Benedick–Beatrice plot are harmonized because they are friends

    2. The Claudio–Hero plot and the Benedick–Beatrice plot are harmonized because they are both love stories

    3. The Claudio–Hero and the Benedick–Beatrice plot are both harmonized by their gaiety until crisis occurs

  B. Polarization of plots

    1. The polarization of the plots begin when reflective Benedick will no longer play court jester for Claudio and Don Pedro

    2. The crisis in the Claudio–Hero plot, the refusal and accusal of Hero, precipitates an extended crisis in the Benedick–Beatrice plot

    3. The crisis in the Benedick–Beatrice plot, Beatrice's demand that Benedick kill Claudio, accelerates the polarization between the two plots

    4. The two plots are completely polarized when Benedick agrees to, and then challenges, Claudio

  C. Reconciliation of plots

    1. The Claudio–Hero plot is reconciled with the Benedick–Beatrice plot when Benedick releases penitent Claudio from his challenge

    2. The Claudio–Hero plot is reconciled with the Beatrice–Benedick plot as both couples prepare for their double-wedding

V. Conclusion: Shakespeare uses parallels and counterpoints to interweave two love stories, one based on convention, the other on invention, in a pattern that begins in harmony, splits in crisis, and resolves in reconciliation.

Topic #2

Appearance versus reality is the major theme in *Much Ado About Nothing* and the lesson of the play is to learn to discriminate properly and to estimate everything at its true value. Write an analytical essay on misnotings that take place in this play, as well as the way in which they are resolved; include the motifs, imagery, dialogue, and theatrical devices that Shakespeare employs to explore this theme.

Outline

I. Thesis Statement: *In* Much Ado About Nothing, *Shakespeare explores the theme of appearance versus reality and its lesson— proper discrimination and true value estimation—through a series of deceptions, emphasized by mask motifs and fashion imagery, which are resolved as the characters are willing to perceive the truth.*

II. Appearance versus reality brought about by a series of deceptions

    A. Benign deceptions

        1. The servant of Antonio overheard a conversation that concerned his master's niece and he shared it with him

        2. The friends of Benedick and Beatrice gulled them into believing each loved the other

        3. Friar Francis suggested that Leonato tell everyone his daughter Hero died until her name was cleared

        4. Leonato tests Claudio's contrition with the penance of mourning at the tomb and marrying his niece, sight unseen

    B. Malicious deceptions

        1. Don John deceived Claudio into believing that his friend Don Pedro wooed Hero for himself

        2. Don John and Borachio deceived Claudio and Don Pedro into believing that Hero was a wanton

III. Appearance versus reality emphasized with mask motifs

   A. Social masks

     1. The pointed wordspar between Benedick and Beatrice is a mask for their real feelings for each other

     2. The decorus language of the aristocrats masks their real feelings and thoughts, which are hidden beneath their words

     3. Dogberry uses high–faluting words he doesn't understand to impress others

   B. Actual masks

     1. The men wear actual masks at the masquerade ball to purposefully deceive each other

     2. Margaret wears Hero's clothing to pretend she is Hero

     3. The women wear masks in the denouement to hide their identities from their future husbands

IV. Appearance versus reality stressed with fashion imagery

   A. Dialogue

     1. Beatrice uses fashion imagery to describe Benedick

     2. Benedick uses fashion imagery to describe Beatrice

     3. Claudio and Don Pedro use fashion imagery to describe Benedick

     4. Borachio uses fashion imagery to introduce his tale of villainy to Conrade

     5. Benedick uses fashion imagery to describe his freedom from another man's opinion

   B. Costumes

     1. Claudio is dressed as a groom although he intends to renounce Hero

     2. Dogberry is dressed as a magistrate for his examination of the prisoners although he has not studied law

V. Appearance versus reality is resolved through recognizing the truth

   A. Proper discrimination

      1. Claudio recognizes his error of mistaking, and Hero recognizes she was wronged only as long as she was slandered

      2. Benedick and Beatrice both recognize the depth of their feelings for each other

   B. Estimating true value

      1. Claudio and Hero recognize that their relationship must begin with trust and faith

      2. Benedick and Beatrice recognize that their love for each other has more value than their friends' opinions of them

VI. Conclusion: Willingness to see the truth gives the proper discrimination and estimation of true value to see past deceptions, and is emphasized in *Much Ado About Nothing* with mask motifs and fashion imagery.

Topic #3

In *Much Ado About Nothing*, Benedick and Beatrice explore an unconventional path of love. Write an analytical essay on the lovers' journey in awareness, and the way in which Shakespeare uses syntactic structures to reflect this movement.

Outline

I. Thesis Statement: *Benedick and Beatrice explore an unconventional path of love; a journey in awareness which is reflected in their syntactic expression.*

II. Unconventional path of love

   A. Refuse to comply

      1. Benedick and Beatrice are contemptuous of convention

      2.   Benedick and Beatrice are marriage–bashers

   B.   Follow their ideals

      1.   Benedick and Beatrice spontaneously explore their relationship

      2.   Benedick and Beatrice commit to a true union

III.   Journey in awareness

   A.   Point of departure

      1.   Benedick and Beatrice mask their feelings

      2.   Benedick and Beatrice have an adversarial relationship

      3.   Benedick and Beatrice are locked in past memories

      4.   Benedick and Beatrice are negatively obsessed with each other

   B.   Change of course

      1.   Benedick and Beatrice recognize their true feelings for each other

      2.   Benedick and Beatrice recognize their faults and resolve to mend their ways

      3.   Benedick and Beatrice see each other with a fresh viewpoint

      4.   Benedick and Beatrice are truly concerned about each other

   C.   Arrival

      1.   Benedick and Beatrice express their feelings and confess their love for one another

      2.   Benedick and Beatrice work in harmony

      3.   Benedick and Beatrice openly explore each other

      4.   Benedick and Beatrice unite and their joy flows out to others

IV.   Syntactic change of expression

   A.   Begins

    1. Benedick and Beatrice camouflage their feelings with clever banter

    2. Benedick and Beatrice wordspar for intellectual supremacy

    3. Benedick and Beatrice speak elaborately for oblique rhetorical effect on others

  B. Changes

    1. Benedick and Beatrice restrain themselves during their parallel gulling scenes

    2. Benedick and Beatrice, in soliloquies, change their speech patterns as they change their intentions toward each other

  C. Ends

    1. Benedick and Beatrice express their feelings

    2. Benedick and Beatrice good naturedly tease each other and harmonize their wit

    3. Benedick and Beatrice are true to themselves and speak directly from their hearts

V. Conclusion: Benedick and Beatrice's unconventional path of love took them on a journey in which they recognized and surrendered their false verbal masks and found their true voices.

Topic #4

Shakespeare uses off stage action in the plot structure of *Much Ado About Nothing.* Write an essay, analyzing the types of offstage action employed and its value to the play.

Outline

I. Thesis Statement: *Shakespeare employs valuable types of off stage action in his play,* Much Ado About Nothing.

II. Types of off stage action

  A. Conversations

    1.   Antonio's servant overhears Claudio and Don Pedro

    2.   Benedick and Beatrice begin their conversation before we hear their dialogue at the masked ball

  B. Actions

    1.   Don John, Claudio, and Don Pedro witness the staged deceit to slander Hero

    2.   Leonato conducts a formal examination of persons involved in the slander

III. Value of off stage action

  A. Information

    1.   Shakespeare keeps us informed of truths the players are not privy to

    2.   Shakespeare keeps our imaginations working so that we participate as active observers

  B. Movement of action

    1.   Shakespeare dynamically uses off stage action to condense the action of the play

    2.   Shakespeare economically uses off stage action for emphasis

    3.   Shakespeare uses off stage action for tonal changes

IV. Conclusion: The different types of off stage action that Shakespeare uses in *Much Ado About Nothing* are necessary for information and movement of action.

SECTION EIGHT

Bibliography

Quotations from *Much Ado About Nothing* are taken from the following translation.

Bevington, David, ed. *Much Ado About Nothing*. New York: Bantam Books, 1988. Foreword written by Joseph Papp.

Other Sources

Barish, Jonas A. *Pattern and Purpose in the Prose of Much Ado About Nothing*. Rice University Studies, 60:2, 1974, pp. 19–30.

Berry, Ralph. Mu*ch Ado About Nothing: Structure & Texture*. English Studies 52, 1971, pp. 211–223.

Fillmore, Charles. Me*taphysical Bible Dictionary*, Missouri: Unity, 1931.

Furness, Horace Howard, ed. *Much Ado About Nothing, A New Variorum Edition of Shakespeare*. New York: Dover Publications, Inc., 1964.

Gaskell, G.A. *Dictionary of all Scriptures and Myths*. New York: Julian Press, Inc., 1973.

Hockey, Dorothy C. *Notes Notes, Forsooth....* Shakespeare Quarterly 8, 1957, pp. 353–358. Delineates the pattern of misnoting or false noting as the thematic device of the play.

Holy Bible, Philadelphia: National Bible Press, conformable to the edition of 1611 commonly known as the King James Version.

Owen, Charles A., Jr. *Comic Awareness, Style, and Dramatic Technique in Much Ado About Nothing.* Boston University Studies in English, Vol. 5, No. 4, Winter 1961, pp. 193–207.

Quiller–Couch, Sir Arthur and John Dover Wilson, ed. *Much Ado About Nothing, The Works of Shakespeare.* London:Cambridge University Press, 1969.

Shaw, George Bernard. *Our Theatres in the Nineties.* 3 vols. London: Constable & Co., Ltd., 1932.

Skeat, Rev. Walter W. *A Concise Etymological Dictionary of the English Language.* New York: Capricorn Books, 1963.

Stauffer, Donald A. *Shakespeare's World of Images.* New York: W.W. Norton and Company, Inc., 1949.

Stevenson, David L., ed. M*uch Ado About Nothing.* New York: Signet, 1964.

Swinburne, Algernon Charles. *A Study of Shakespeare.* London 1880.

Wey, James J. *"To Grace Harmony": Musical Design in Much Ado About Nothing.* Boston University Studies in English, Vol. IV, No. 3, Autumn 1960, pp. 181–188.

REA's Test Preps
The Best in Test Preparation

- REA "Test Preps" are far **more** comprehensive than any other test preparation series
- Each book contains up to **eight** full-length practice exams based on the most recent exams
- **Every** type of question likely to be given on the exams is included
- Answers are accompanied by **full** and **detailed** explanations

REA has published over 60 Test Preparation volumes in several series. They include:

Advanced Placement Exams (APs)
Biology
Calculus AB & Calculus BC
Chemistry
Computer Science
English Language & Composition
English Literature & Composition
European History
Government & Politics
Physics
Psychology
Spanish Language
United States History

College Level Examination Program (CLEP)
American History I
Analysis & Interpretation of Literature
College Algebra
Freshman College Composition
General Examinations
Human Growth and Development
Introductory Sociology
Principles of Marketing

SAT II: Subject Tests
American History
Biology
Chemistry
French
German
Literature

SAT II: Subject Tests (continued)
Mathematics Level IC, IIC
Physics
Spanish
Writing

Graduate Record Exams (GREs)
Biology
Chemistry
Computer Science
Economics
Engineering
General
History
Literature in English
Mathematics
Physics
Political Science
Psychology
Sociology

ACT - American College Testing Assessment

ASVAB - Armed Service Vocational Aptitude Battery

CBEST - California Basic Educational Skills Test

CDL - Commercial Driver's License Exam

CLAST - College Level Academic Skills Test

ELM - Entry Level Mathematics

ExCET - Exam for Certification of Educators in Texas

FE (EIT) - Fundamentals of Engineering Exam

FE Review - Fundamentals of Engineering Review

GED - High School Equivalency Diploma Exam (US & Canadian editions)

GMAT - Graduate Management Admission Test

LSAT - Law School Admission Test

MAT - Miller Analogies Test

MCAT - Medical College Admission Test

MSAT - Multiple Subjects Assessment for Teachers

NTE - National Teachers Exam

PPST - Pre-Professional Skills Tests

PSAT - Preliminary Scholastic Assessment Test

SAT I - Reasoning Test

SAT I - Quick Study & Review

TASP - Texas Academic Skills Program

TOEFL - Test of English as a Foreign Language

RESEARCH & EDUCATION ASSOCIATION
61 Ethel Road W. • Piscataway, New Jersey 08854
Phone: (908) 819-8880

Please send me more information about your Test Prep Books

Name _____

Address _____

City _____ State _____ Zip _____

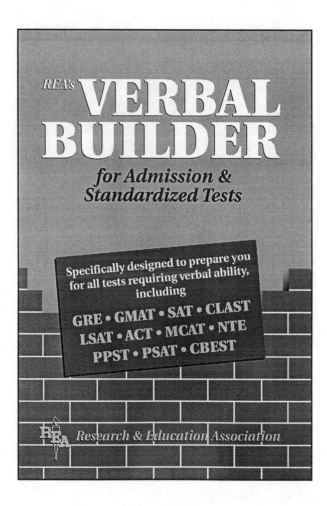

Available at your local bookstore or order directly from us by sending in coupon below.

MAXnotes®

REA's Literature Study Guides

MAXnotes® are student-friendly. They offer a fresh look at masterpieces of literature, presented in a lively and interesting fashion. **MAXnotes®** offer the essentials of what you should know about the work, including outlines, explanations and discussions of the plot, character lists, analyses, and historical context. **MAXnotes®** are designed to help you think independently about literary works by raising various issues and thought-provoking ideas and questions. Written by literary experts who currently teach the subject, **MAXnotes®** enhance your understanding and enjoyment of the work.

Available **MAXnotes®** include the following:

Absalom, Absalom!	Heart of Darkness	Of Mice and Men
The Aeneid of Virgil	Henry IV, Part I	On the Road
Animal Farm	Henry V	Othello
Antony and Cleopatra	The House on Mango Street	Paradise Lost
As I Lay Dying	Huckleberry Finn	A Passage to India
As You Like It	I Know Why the Caged	Plato's Republic
The Autobiography of	Bird Sings	Portrait of a Lady
Malcolm X	The Iliad	A Portrait of the Artist
The Awakening	Invisible Man	as a Young Man
Beloved	Jane Eyre	Pride and Prejudice
Beowulf	Jazz	A Raisin in the Sun
Billy Budd	The Joy Luck Club	Richard II
The Bluest Eye, A Novel	Jude the Obscure	Romeo and Juliet
Brave New World	Julius Caesar	The Scarlet Letter
The Canterbury Tales	King Lear	Sir Gawain and the
The Catcher in the Rye	Les Misérables	Green Knight
The Color Purple	Lord of the Flies	Slaughterhouse-Five
The Crucible	Macbeth	Song of Solomon
Death in Venice	The Merchant of Venice	The Sound and the Fury
Death of a Salesman	The Metamorphoses of Ovid	The Stranger
The Divine Comedy I: Inferno	The Metamorphosis	The Sun Also Rises
Dubliners	Middlemarch	A Tale of Two Cities
Emma	A Midsummer Night's Dream	Taming of the Shrew
Euripedes' Electra & Medea	Moby-Dick	The Tempest
Frankenstein	Moll Flanders	Tess of the D'Urbervilles
Gone with the Wind	Mrs. Dalloway	Their Eyes Were Watching God
The Grapes of Wrath	Much Ado About Nothing	To Kill a Mockingbird
Great Expectations	My Antonia	To the Lighthouse
The Great Gatsby	Native Son	Twelfth Night
Gulliver's Travels	1984	Uncle Tom's Cabin
Hamlet	The Odyssey	Waiting for Godot
Hard Times	Oedipus Trilogy	Wuthering Heights

RESEARCH & EDUCATION ASSOCIATION
61 Ethel Road W. • Piscataway, New Jersey 08854
Phone: (908) 819-8880

Please send me more information about MAXnotes®.

Name _____

Address _____

City _____ State _____ Zip _____